The Power2BU!

The ABCs of Life Enrichment
Personal Empowerment Strategies

By

Thomas Abdul-Salaam
thepower2bu@yahoo.com

For general information on other products and services please contact Thomas Abdul-Salaam at www.thepower2bu.com. *For more information about The Power 2BU! Workshops, Television Programs, and other products visit our web site at* www.thepower2bu.com.

Library of Congress Cataloging-in-Publication Data:

Abdul-Salaam, Thomas, 1953 -
    The Power 2BU!: The ABCs of Life Enrichment / Thomas Abdul-
    Salaam.

    Includes bibliographical references and index.
    ISBN-13: 978-0-6152-1740-6

Printed in the United States of America.

The real duty of man is not to extend his power or multiply his wealth beyond his needs, but to enrich and enjoy his imperishable possession his soul. -- Gilbert Highet

Table of Contents

Acknowledgments

With the name of God, The Merciful, The Redeemer, I want to acknowledge all of the kinships I owe thanks in my effort to bring forth *The ABC's Of Life Enrichment Personal Empowerment Tips.* Nothing is done solely by one's self. It takes a team effort 2BU! I have had help and gotten advice prior to writing what I hope to be my first of many books to come.

The first person I owe thanks to is my wife and friend of 20 years, Aisha Kareem, PhD. Without your support over the many years I would not have been enriched. I am equally proud of U and your many accomplishments as an educator. Thanks for the years! I love U!!!

Faheem Hameed, U have been a dear friend and true brother for over 30 years. Your help on this book was invaluable. Thank U for the time to proof read and edit this book. Friends like U are rare and hard to find. But who's looking! To your lovely wife, Feyral, thanks U for your patience in this matter.

The cover and logo was designed by my niece, Raquel Jimenez-Stanley who came to her uncle's aid without hesitation. I am in your debt! To my Nephew, Robbie, I appreciate U letting me borrow your wife's time when I know U and the children needed her. May God bless U and your young family with much success.

All of this would not be real, if it was not for all of the Life Enrichment Tip (etips) readers. Your comments have been heart-felt. Most of U I have never met but I feel a kinship with U. Thank U for your readership and continued support as we enter our third year.

Next, I want to thank Michael Port of the 'Think Big Revolution' (www.MichaelPort.com) for all of the advise and encouragement U offer every week. As one of my wife's favorite poems reads, "When U thought I was not looking..." well, I was looking and I am still listening.

If it had not been for the many clients who gave me an opportunity to practice my skills, I would just be a 'wanna be', hoping and wishing. Great lessons have come from our many encounters. U trusted me and gave me the chance to become more proficient in the art of Life Enrichment.

To my mother, Willie Lee Smith-Williams, and my father, Billy Else Williams, while U are no longer with me, I dedicate this book in your memory. If any one has enriched my life, it is U! All of the straight talk, tough love, and encouragement 2BMe! **I LOVE U!**

I would like to also dedicate this book to my Uncle, John Smith, my mother's brother. He passed away May 16, 2008 just as I was submitting this book for review. U were the last connection to the past. From God we come and to God we are returning!

Forward

It should come as no surprise to anyone that today, more so than any time in the history of civilization, has the search for meaning, elevating one's self-awareness and finding purpose to one's life been so desperately sought after. Yet, is it any wonder? Our world has become one in which we define ourselves in terms of our many roles or social masks. We define ourselves in terms of what we *do* as opposed to who we *are* or who we are *becoming.* We engage one another by initially describing what it is we do for a living such as, "I'm the CEO of XYZ Company", "I teach fifth graders", "I work at the University" and so on.

Over time, thoughts, actions and behaviors become trained to support superficial and insignificant social roles which have been erected to shield our authentic inner core, which is the essence of our being. In times of perceived danger these same thoughts are engaged to defend one's egoist mind which provides, at best, a transient sense of relief. While this type of existence may translate into temporarily enhancing a sense of self, it also serves as the catalyst for alienation. It instills a sense of superiority over others on one extreme and seeing self as a victim on the other. In a collective sense, it creates an "us versus them" mentality. If it is understood that we all have arrived from the same universal source, this sense of being disconnected from others, only serves to defy the natural order of the universe and keeps us in a state of separation not only from others but from our authentic Self. It lacks life enrichment!

The Power 2BU! provides the reader with insight and the tools needed to elevate beyond learned limitations. It provides both reflection and tools that support your desire to move towards becoming *who you really are*. This book, The *ABCs of Life Enrichment*, offers very real and practical tools on how *2BU!* Regardless of your present situation or circumstances which have brought you to where you are, *The Power 2BU!* provides you with a tool kit to help identify those conditions which block personal growth. The tools will guide your desire to become who you deserve 2B. Thomas has effectively integrated his knowledge and experience as a motivator, coach and spiritual leader in a thought provoking manner that will inspire readers of all ages to achieve higher levels of consciousness and self-awareness.

Imagine a new level of existence where you no longer hide behind social roles and masks. Imagine further that your life is no longer dictated by the approval of external sources. Instead, your life is enriched by an internal force that allows you *2BU!* Therefore experience more joy and meaning than you *do now*. You recognize that your own definition of who you are is more vibrant than titles and richer then what you possess. Your renewed self-awareness is inspired to the point you know at your core you have attained *The Power 2BU!*

John P. Carvana, CLCC
Career & Life Purpose Coach
www.DiscoveredPurpose.com

Author's Notes

I was attending a retreat with a human resource organization as a board member and after it was over, the facilitator came up to me and asked me if I had ever heard of executive coaching, I had not. She invited me to learn more about it and concluded her remarks with, "U will make a fine coach."

I attended Executive Coaching training and practiced part-time for nearly three years, until August 2004, when I was terminated. Yes, I was let go! If U are surprised, think of how I felt. I had bills to pay! With the support of my wife, I set up shop at home. We took it as an opportunity to stop just hoping and wishing for someday to arrive.

Getting clients and marketing was no laughing matter. I received an email one day from a man name Michael Port. He offered a free teleconference call which I joined. Immediately, I liked his spirit and approach. Every Monday, I was on his call listening and taking notes. Inspiration was gained from these calls to create Life Enrichment Tips (etips).

Life Enrichment is the central theme of The Power 2BU! This book is a collection of my daily column, Life Enrichment Tips (et*ips) and* distributed via email to 400 plus subscribers. They are written as one half of a conversation, always starting with a quote and the statement, I was just saying...

During my days as a Human Resource Director, to people who were dissatisfied with their job, I would offer what I called a chance to "enrich' their experience. Enrichment is not changing the job but adjusting the boundaries, for empowerment on the job - more decision-making, flexibility, and committee membership, while never compromising safety. Organizational justice, if U will.

I have come to embrace as a frame work, Appreciative Inquiry. I firmly believe in the best of U, that U have a good heart, and U want to do right, despite the present-day status of your lifestyle. A CEO, manager, teacher, youth, or those behind bars all desire a quality lifestyle. The challenge is discovering the authentic U. Establishing the resilience 2BU! in the face of adversities, temptations which test your principles, values, and character. All of us are challenged in life on one level or another.

Your life can be enriched! The quality of your life, the lifestyle you choose is in your hands. *The ABCs of Life Enrichment Personal Empowerment Tips are* a collection of tools assembled to help get the best out of your life by first mastering the ability 2BU! Life can be hard, and it is even harder, when U are 'off' being someone else. Doing things that serve U not! That tears at the very fabric of The Power 2BU!

The Power 2BU! helps U pursue your earthly purpose while not sacrificing your heavenly mission. I hope U enjoy the etips collected in the first of many, The Power 2BU! Handbooks.

Preface

Life Enrichment is about the things, people and experiences that make U a better U. How do U manage the day-to-day challenges of becoming the person U want 2B! The process assumes that U, like most others, need fine tuning, minor adjustments, and an occasional spiritual-social evolution tune up over the span of your lifetime.

It is similar to home repairs that U perform from time to time. U might replace the carpet; U might redesign your kitchen or need to expand the structure of the house. U love your house, i.e. your life, but the neighborhood, the kinships change. Life is like that, U mature, develop, and new experiences leave U with new perspectives. This is life enrichment. Life, past and present, has given U a more enriched point of view. It is a struggle 2BU! with all of your flaws, faults, and fallacies and all the while U have to manage the ups and downs, the slips and falls, and the fame and shame of life 2BU!

The ABC's of Life Enrichment Tips are a tool box, not a step-by-step guide. Each tool is packaged separately. U can read this book from the middle out or back to front but to maximize your potential instantly, I recommend U sit down and read the book cover to cover. See how the tools compliment each other. Stop and spend as much time as U need with a particular tool. Remember, The Power 2BU! is not trying to change U. Enrichment is about the quality of life U wish to live and the person U wish 2B. As my father said on the day of his death, "The quality of my life is more important to me than the quantity of my life." No matter how long U live, The Power 2BU! want it to be a quality life. An authentic life!

When I speak of The Power 2BNew! I am not talking about change. What I want my readers and clients to do is develop the resilience to live the life he or she wants. I don't want U to change what U are doing but think about how/what U are doing, believing, or the direction U are traveling. Is it getting U closer to that quality, authentic life U dream about? Are U compromising the authentic U, your values, principles, and character, which runs against the grain of who U really are inside? U decide if the authentic U is in front of U or lay in another direction.

By the way, The Power 2BU! encourage U to dream and dream often. Dreams are essential to empowering U, 2BU! All that U are and will become is contained in your dreams. So make them quality, authentic dreams. By whatever name U call it - hope, goals, wishes, desires, mission, or purpose. I mean exactly that when I say dream! Dreams give U the resilience to endure the detours, setbacks, and renovations in life required to live an authentic lifestyle.

Life Enrichment is the inner workings of The Power 2BU! One of the tools in the box is to discover, dream and design your own destiny, which is the goal of The Power 2BU! In my talks, trainings, and coaching, I promise that "U can and U will" discover, dream and design your own destiny. Recently, there was a lady name Natalie, she told me up-front "I have never dreamed." Meaning she had no vision, goal or purpose. I repeated my promise to her. By the end of the workshop, Natalie had a dream for herself and was truly enriched by the process. Here is what Natalie wrote, "This workshop for me is more real, and it reached down inside of me, opened doors, and helped me to really see that I can influence my own life." The Power 2BU! gives U the tools to "influence" your own life in real ways. *The ABC's of Life Enrichment* are the tools by which U begin to influence U, 2BU! 2BAuthentic! 2BResilient! Ask yourself these 2BU! questions:

A) Name my top three personal goals?

B) Why am I so committed to my top three goals?

C) What type of person must I become to achieve what I want?

D) What are my greatest fears about success?

E) What do I know about me that holds me back?

F) What do I value most in my life?

G) What are my guiding principles in life?

H) What three character traits define me?

If U keep asking self these questions *The ABC's of life Enrichment* will help U 2BU!
It's a Great Day 2BU!

Thomas Abdul-Salaam
Twin Servant of Peace

Gentle humor and accessible language make this an easy-going guidebook (tool kit) to a life well-lived. Each chapter contains the simple wisdom of spiritual truth, the kind we already know in our hearts, but maybe haven't applied to our lives as fully as we could. Thomas Abdul-Salaam gives us an opportunity to look more deeply at the most human of all questions: how to live a meaningful and happy life. My advice to readers is to take it in and enjoy! -- Toni Mandara Williams, Life Coach, Personal Pathways, pathwayscoach9@yahoo.com

Attitude Is Everything!

"There is very little difference in people. But that little difference makes a big difference. The little difference is attitude. The big difference is whether it is positive or negative." -- W. Clement Stone

I was just saying...

Attitude is like opinions, everybody has one. The difference is whether is it is positive or negative! Your attitude is the window through which U watch life go by. This window filters and shades your perspective on all that U see. How U interpret, respond, and what U think is all colored by attitude. All of the pictures that pass before your eyes get it definition from attitude.

Two boys can grow up in the same house, have the same parents, and walk to the same school, yet one sees his future as positive, while the other sees all of the broke glass, dope dealers, and have no hope at all. The difference is Attitude! Two girls can start off walking through a meadow of flowers and one hates the walk in the "middle of no where", while the other girl is enjoying every step and is in no hurry to get home. Attitude!

There is very little difference between people, but the BIG difference is whether their attitude is positive or negative. The Power 2BU! hinges on which way your attitude swings. If your life is traveling south but your attitude is headed north, U will be alright, even if U hit rock bottom. Remember the movie, "Pursuit of Happyness", Mr. Gardner's life was moving south, his wife left him with a small child, his equipment was stolen, and he slept in a bathroom, but he never gave up on his dream or himself. His attitude was positive, his actions were positive, and his behavior never led to self-sabotage. The difference between him and everyone else was a positive attitude.

As U walk through life, your silent partner is attitude. He will never take the blame and he will never feel sorry for U, even though he is 80 percent of the problem. He will join U in pity parties and enjoy sleeping in late. It rest on your shoulders to whip this guy into shape. Attitude is as positive as U forces him to be. Make him a team player, a contributing partner, and fully accountable for your outlook on life. Positive or negative, it is your choice.

I heard a teacher instruct a group of students on their way to science camp, "wear your hat in the direction U want your life to go." Attitude is about direction! Your attitude give others a hint as to the direction your life is headed. U need to wear your hat in the direction U want your life to go. Life is funny; it works better when it has direction. Life is impressionable like a little child; U can influence your life to go in any direction U want. It is your choice! Right or Left? Up or down? Don't get up each morning and go in whatever direction the wind blows.

Attitude is everything! Attitude is the first portal of enrichment. All things begin with attitude, it affects your direction, vision, and countless other things.

I heard once that everybody's DNA is 97 percent the same. It did not matter whether U were black or white, red or yellow, short or tall, thin or fat, nor rich or poor, there is only 3 percent of separation between U and the next person. Think of attitude as that 3 percent of separation. It's very little but that little difference makes a BIG difference in the race for the gold medal...2BU!

Dare To Believe!

"Believe that U will succeed. Believe it firmly, and U will then do what is necessary to bring success about." – Dale Carnegie

I was just saying...

U have to become a "new" person if what U want is really what U want. U have to believe in what U want to the point that U "bring about" a new set of circumstances to accomplish your dreams. Who U are today is not "big" enough to hand U what U want. If it was so, U would have what U want.

Dale Carnegie says, "...then U will do what is necessary to bring success about." The new U maybe one seminar away from being the person required to bring success about. U may discover a little fine tuning will bring about success.

Most of us are not willing to bring about success. We do not have the belief in our success firmly enough to deliver. It takes a firm belief to go to work on a dream that only U seem to have any emotional connection with. If U maintain a positive attitude aided by a firm belief then "bringing about" success will generate the resilience to succeed.

The Power 2BU! is causing, producing, or giving rise to a more resilient U. It is not always about large changes in your life. Small enrichment can make a big difference. Three pounds lose could be all U need right now to keep the motivation to succeed. Yes, twenty pounds is your goal but U feel better with three pounds gone.

Dare to believe in U! Belief can hold U back or propel U forward. What U believe and how U believe it has a major impact on your attitude. If U believe this is a "dog eat dog" world then it will affect your attitude. What do U believe? Is the golden rule "he who has the gold makes the rules" or "do unto others as U want done unto U." Can U see how belief can shape your attitude? The first belief will have U living life opposite of the person who believes the latter. Both of U will have an entirely different attitude about the same thing, the golden rule. How U each applies it in your life will affect how U bring about success.

Bring about success is a combination of belief and attitude. U have to know what U believe, then believe it to the point that U trust it with your life. U must have faith in your perspective on the golden rule as being the best belief for your life's direction. If U find your direction and beliefs are not working for U, dare to correct your beliefs. Find new ones that will bring about success. Don't think U have to hold to the same set of beliefs all the days of your life. As U mature, have new experiences, and meet new people your beliefs may need adjusting a little. It's not a bad thing to reexamine your beliefs. Look how advances in technology have altered beliefs.

Give yourself a fighting chance to succeed. Dare to believe in The Power 2BU!

Commitment:
Accept No Excuses!

"There is a difference between interest and commitment. When you're interested in doing something, you do it only when it's convenient. When you're committed to something, you accept no excuses; only results." -- Kenneth Blanchard

I was just saying...

U normally have more interest than U have commitment. Your plate is full of things to do. If U cataloged into columns your commitment list would be shorter than your interest list.

2BCommitted takes too much commitment! U do your life a disservice to over-commit yourself. Commitment is too complete and all encompassing to try and execute more than two or three things at a time. Put the other things on your interest plate.

Knowing the difference between the two could save U false-starts, bouts of procrastination, and the fear of completion. U are not a procrastinator, U have yet to divide your plate into the commitment list and the interest list. The more U attempt to work off of your interest list, the more U define yourself as lazy, unworthy of success, and a loser. U are not any of those things, but U are confused about the things U are really committed to complete.

Look for signs of commitment. When U prefer to do it more than the other things on your plate it is most likely a good sign. If U can truly envision the results, U just might be committed to it. Commitment in some cases, involuntary, U find yourself moved or inspired to proceed, plan, and keep on pushing forward. Your work shows high attention to detail, your performance is seeking new levels of results, and your dreams are clearer than before. Commitment is a life enrichment experience.

When U discover where your commitment lies, the realization alone will enrich your life.   The new attitude, the new belief, and a new commitment will automatically produce The Power 2BU! U will feel the instant it happens.   Purpose is born out of commitment. U become more loyal and steadfast. U are no longer a person without direction or a mission in life. Your commitments define your existence. From that moment, U are new, born again with the resilience 2BNew!

The potency 2BU! is discovered in your commitments. U are more effective when U can separate your interests from your commitments. 2BU! is powerful but it takes commitment 2BU! Commitment takes 100 percent commitment 2U, 2BU!

Discover, Dream & Design
Your Destiny!

"I have no doubt whatever that most people live, whether physically, intellectually, or morally, in a very restricted circle of their potential being...we all have reservoirs of life to draw upon of which we do not dream." -- Dr. William James

I was just saying...

U are the most underutilized of all of God's creation. A breath of life was breathed into U on the day U was born which is a force U are yet to reckon with. The potential in U is greater than all of the mechanical machines, computers, and GPS satellites U build. U give more attention to discovering, dreaming and designing "things" than U do to your own destiny.

U were born to discover who, what, where, why, and how of life...your life. Discovery is the first purpose of human life. U come here blank, void of knowledge, understanding, or skills. The breath of life gave U the ability to discover and explore the environment which U are born into. It is this environment and your interaction with it which will have a long lasting impression upon U. Discovery leads to beliefs, commitments, and attitudes that go into the makings of U!

Next, your discoveries give rise to dreams. Insight, hopes, and purpose is gained from dreams. Dreams are the stepping stones to your potential. Dreams open up your potential 2BNew! What U dream about leaves impressions upon your soul. Dreams can lead to fears or cheers. U can fear yourself or U can cheer self. When U fear your 'light', U make excuses for yourself, U move to the 'dark side' of life. Your fears short circuit your intellectual, physical, and moral potential, cheating U of life by settling for pieces of a dream. If U discover the real Power 2BU, dreams 2BU come at U a hundred miles per hour. Ideas, imaginations, innovations and the like are part of the cheering process. Your own potential can be very overwhelming but don't be afraid 2BU! Embrace yourself, show yourself love and respect your dreams.

Once U can harness the power to dream, U can begin the design process of life enrichment. Design involves plans, processes, and strategies for framing the future. U must be able to capture the dreams by way of painting, drawing, and speaking to the vision. U need to believe before U can sell your illustration of the future to others. U have to believe in the dream enough to bring it about. It is vital that U become a romanticist and fall in love with your designs, the futurist U. Create the attitude and commitment to your dreams required to bring about The Power 2BNew!

Discovery, dreams, and design reveal your destiny. Your destiny is in your hands, mind and heart. Purpose is yours 2Discover, 2Dream, and 2Design. U have no destiny until U give self a destiny. If U start at three years old believing, forming the attitude, and the commitment to be a singer, doctor, or basketball player...Yes, it will feel like U were "born" to do just that one thing. U are not born to do this or that. U are born 2Discover, 2Dream, and 2Design your Destiny!

The breath of life breathe into U, gave U the ability to create your purpose. U can be all that U wish to be. U can change courses in the middle of the river as often as U wish. If the direction U are traveling today is not working for U then find a new one that does. STOP and discover, dream, and design a destiny 2BU! This will give U The Power 2BNew!

The goal of The Power 2BU! is 2Discover, 2Dream, and 2Design your destiny 2BNew!

The Fire of Enthusiasm!

"We act as though comfort and luxury were the chief requirements of life, when all that we need to make us happy is something to be enthusiastic about." -- Charles Kingsley

I was just saying...

Enthusiasm is your attitude on fire. It is commitment in action. Enthusiasm is the turbo booster of The Power 2BU!

If U are not enthusiastic about being U, your spirit will turn gray long before the hair on your head. The soul longs for something 2BPassionate about, a dream that lights up all of the dark corners of the heart, a dream so powerful it forces U to think and rethink and push U to commit. Enthusiasm is priceless in your pursuit 2BU! If U fail 2BExcited about being U, then U will be missing in action all the days of your life. Enthusiasm will help U get a life...enriched

Enthusiasm comes from the Greek roots en and theos and means "God within." U have been given the spirit of God through the breath of life. Enthusiasm is innate to every human being, it is not in some of us, it is in all of us. U have to tap into enthusiasm to gain The Power 2BU! When U discover the spirit of passion, U will feel enriched, alive, and blessed. The comforts and luxuries of life will fade in comparison to the joy of the fire of enthusiasm.

U may have felt passionate at periods of your life but it is not enough to be enthusiastic for short periods of time. U should to learn how to hold on to the spirit of enthusiasm and turn it into a barn fire within U. Even in the face of adversities, U should be enthusiastic about the moment and what is yet to come. U can keep your head up when falsely accused, judged, and sentenced. If U are kept in solitary confinement for 25 years of your life, U still emerge passionate. When U emerge, your spirit is emboldened, your dreams are more real, and your destiny shows on your face. Nelson Mendela is such a man. Enthusiasm was his weapon that kept his attitude committed to his principles and values.   Enthusiasm is a main ingredient in The Power 2BU!

2BNew! is sparked by enthusiasm. The pursuit 2BU! is not found in comforts and luxuries but in discovering the "God within." Never give up on finding yourself, knowing yourself, and The Power 2BU! The power to find happiness will enrich your life within and without.

The Bosom of Forgiveness!

"Love lets the past die. It moves people to a new beginning without settling the past. Love prefers to tuck the loose ends of past rights and wrongs in the bosom of forgiveness, and pushes us into a new start." -- Lewis B. Smedes

I was just saying...

Forgiveness is one of the most important tools U have in The Power 2BU! tool box. It is an instrument U should reach for often. Give yourself the gift of forgiveness!

U can gain long term benefits from the act of self-forgiveness. U are not perfect and never will be. U are human and humans need to forgive and move on...everyday! Relax on taking yourself to the barn for one of those famous "come to Jesus" meetings. Let love and forgiveness work for U more often.

The Power 2BU! hinges on forgiveness. If U fail to forgive self and others, U fail to love self and others. When U can push pass mistakes, wrongs, and character flaws U serve your mental and spiritual well-being. To forgive is human, it is essential that humans learn to forgive just to maintain a sense of sanity. Forgiveness is the tool U use to bridge the gap between who U are and the person U hope to be. If U fail to give the present-day U a break, U will never arrive at the person U wish 2B.

Life only gets better once U forgive. Without it your mind and spirit seeks to sabotage its own efforts. Fear rises to the leadership position. U become a disbeliever in self. Your enthusiasm is hampered. Decisions become harder to make. Your life spirals downward into recovery verses discovery, confusion, and negative self-talk. When all U have to do is reach into you're Power 2BU! tool box for instant relief, F-O-R-G-I-V-E-N-E-S-S!

Never take up residence in the City of Regret. Never throw yourself pity parties. Never make friends with the Done Family...Should Have, Would Have, or Could Have. Avoid guilt trips altogether! Forgiveness will serve U better over the long haul. The City of Regret is not a place for people who want their life back. The Power 2BU! is no where to be found in that dark and dismal place. Remember U can not change yesterday but U can have a major impact on tomorrow if U just forgive self and others.

The Power 2BU! is more achievable with love and forgiveness. New beginnings, new places, new faces, and new spaces stimulate enthusiasm. New experiences, new relationships, and new information can build an attitude 2BU! within your soul beyond measure. 2BNew! is not about settling the past, nor agreeing who is right or wrong, 2BNew! is found in forgiveness of the past. Forgive people who always need to be right and those who always think they are wrong. Start with yourself.

The Power 2BU! is real honest forgiveness. U are the warden of your own prison. The key to the front gate is self-forgiveness. Pardon yourself! Forgive others and live guilt FREE!

Give 2BSignificant!

"Success in life has nothing to do with what you gain in life or accomplish for yourself. It's what you do for others." -- Danny Thomas

I was just saying...

U work all of your life 2BSuccessful and all U end up with is more material things than U can use. U are taught that success is the purpose of life and that anything short of it should depress U. I think success is over rated!

If U really want 2BSuccessful, I would suggest that U work all of your life 2BSignificant. Giving gives U the capacity 2BRemembered.

Charity is the spirit of success. If U were to obey the spirit of success, U would desire to give. Following the 'spirit' of the law is different than the 'word' of the law. Real success is not about the word but the spirit! Success should make U meaningful. U give in a way which empowers the lives of family, friends, and strangers, thereby empowering U, 2BU!

The Power 2BU! is found when U seek 2BSignificant. Your thinking will be affected by this approach. It gives U a different mental process when U set out 2BSuccessful in life. Your character will be transformed 2BProductive, 2BContributing to the overall well-being of the community by paying it forward and giving back.

Giving impacts your whole life, especially if U give away the things that U truly value. If U have billions of dollars, giving money may not affect U as much as giving your time, which U place a greater value on. 2BSignificant requires the giving of something that is significant to U.

Life enrichment is not generated by your struggle 2BSuccessful, it is powered by giving. U feel new, U think new and U do new things when U give. Giving enriches your soul; it puts a smile on your face and benefits others. Giving is symbolic of the kind of person U are or hope 2B. Giving furnishes the hope others need to believe in their own Power 2BNew!

Success Is mainly about one individual achieving, while giving is about the masses. The Power 2BU! is 2BGiving, 2BSignificant, and 2BCharitable in order 2BSuccessful. The Power 2BNew! is an act of reaching out to others and thereby U are enriched knowing that U have touched the lives of family and strangers alike. Your act of giving is a two edge sword, it enriches and it heals. Everyone benefit!

Choose Humor!

"If you could choose one characteristic that would get you through life, choose a sense of humor." -- Jennifer James

I was just saying...

A joke is funny, but humor is a characteristic which can enrich your life. Humor is not about telling a joke or being a comedian. Humor allows U to endure the unexpected, the unconventional, the unpleasant, and the unbearable.

The more humorous your perspective on yourself, the less stressed U will be over your shortcomings. Life is short and the best way to lengthen life is to find humor. Therefore when U look back, many joys will be found which made your time on earth seemed like forever.

If U take self too serious the lessons of life might come harder than they have to. Give yourself a chance to smile when the unexpected happens. Don't curse or hate the moment, discover the lighter side. Don't say, "Sh*t happens." Instead choose a sense of humor about the event. Don't internalize the event as cruel and unusual punishment that U so rightly desired. It is best to let humor carry the day.

Humor is the ability to laugh or poke fun at something or someone which gives less meaning to an unconventional set of circumstances, such as falling out of a chair in the middle of a meeting. U might

17

jump up and say, "Now for the main act, I will disappear." Take on your behavior before others do and if they do, go with the flow, join in and laugh at yourself. Let humor be a characteristic others can expect from U. Remember this is not about telling jokes but being humorous. My mother put this tool in my Power 2BU! tool box.

People tend to enjoy U better when they know U can take one on the chin and keep on ticking.

Humor is like one-liners. They are light, mean no harm, and have a pinch of truth and a twist on the situation. Resist making the person the object but focus on the event itself.

Let humor enrich your journey, your experiences, and your unbearable moments. The Power 2BU! is one laugh away or one unpleasant set of circumstance away. The Power 2BNew! is only one slip, trip, or fall away. Mark the moment with humor!

Imagination Creates Pictures!

"The most interesting people are the people with the most interesting pictures in their minds." --
Earl Nightingale

I was just saying...

One of the main objectives of The Power 2BU! is about creating interesting visions, pictures, and images, dreams if U will, of one's future. The pictures come from your heart...dreams, wishes or inspirations which are fed to the mind to shape and design, i.e. to visualize. The mind is the factory which turn dreams into pictures, words and realities. The Power 2BU! must have imagination to flourish.

One of the goals of The Power 2BU! is to give U the courage to lead with your heart. Your imagination, innovation, and intuition springs from your heart which the mind converts into pictures. It is the heart which received the breath of life. It is the chamber which the "God within", i.e. The Power 2BU! lives. The mind is its help mate. It lays the plans, has the skills, and the ability to synthesis imagination to produce pictures.

Have no doubt about the impact of pictures on your enthusiasm! Without imagination there would be no pictures to guide U to your destiny, purpose or mission 2BSignificant. Your pictures are the beginning of your vision of success. If U cannot produce images then most likely your heart is without enthusiasm to create the imagination, innovation, ideas and inspiration to dream. Life's forward movement is directly related to the imagination of the heart and the mind's capacity to manufacture the pictures which reveal the power of the God within.

Think of it like this, the heart is U, and the mind is the JENIE standing ready to turn your IMAGINATION, wishes, and desires, into PICTURES, reality.

If your mind cannot hold on to the imagination of the heart, the dream is loss. U have to train your mind to capture the inspirations the heart puts forth. It is good practice to write down these personal revelations and work on them as soon as possible. Get in the habit of allowing your heart to speak to the mind and the mind the experience of picturing that which it hears.

It is said, "If U can conceive it, U can achieve it." The mind's role is to achieve what the heart conceives. U need to understand that conception starts in the heart, not in the brain. The Power 2BU! is only as powerful as your heart's connection with your mind. The Power 2BNew! is led by imagination.

Enjoy the Joy!

"Enjoy the journey, enjoy ever moment, and quit worrying about winning and losing." -- Matt Biondi

I was just saying...

The journey should bring U joy. Joy is a state of being happy but when U enjoy, U actually spend quality time with the people, places and things U draw joy from. The Power 2BU! has at its core, joy. Enjoyment puts U on road 2BNew!

If U have to worry about winning and losing then U are not enjoying life. Life can become joyless if time is spent watching the score board every second of the game. If U are counting your money at the table U are already a loser. Keeping up with the Jones' is playing a joyless game. Inventorying your haves and have-nots can take the wind out of your sails. Stop watching the shot clock!

U should be too focused on enjoying the game to count your money at the table. Enjoy the joy! The Power 2BU! is derived from enjoyment. Worry brings about misery, gloom, and rejection of your self-worth. Life is not enriched by score cards or stats; life is better off lived in joy for the total benefit of capturing the bliss of the journey.

U have been taught that winning is everything. Being the last man standing is the purpose of the game. The game is 2BEnjoyed! U win when U find joy! Winning may be your thing. Losing may depress U. Winning is what U live for. U may like rubbing peoples face in your fame. Life would have no meaning to U if winning was no longer an option. Then I say, enjoy winning, enjoy the rush U get from putting another notch in your fence post. If this is U I would be wrong to tell U not to enjoy your pursuit of happiness. But, Let me ask U to look in the mirror and assure yourself that U have not becoming the villain.

For those who like losing, being humble, and careless about score boards and the like in life, I say, make sure U are not playing the role of the victim. U can become quite skillful in the victim role. Losing is your badge of courageous U wear pinned to your lapel. U think the world is a better place because U take the crap U do. Well, while I hope that U find joy in your role, do not let your present-day state lead U to believe that victims get to heaven ahead of everyone else. Not finding The Power 2BU! and not living up to your potential is a crime, if not a sin!

The goal should be to enjoy the journey. Joy moves U toward enrichment, which seeks to guarantee your success neither by winning nor losing but by investing in The Power 2BU! Become vested in U, enjoy U, enjoy the journey and stop worrying about winning and losing. Become invested in your life and enjoy The Power 2BNew!

Kinships R Precious!

"Each contact with a human being is so rare, so precious, one should preserve it." -- Anais Nin

I was just saying...

Interaction is essential to the well-being of humans. Every contact is precious, not only for what U may gain but for what U have to give. The Power 2BU! is enriched through your many associations made while U enjoy the journey.

There are very few individuals that really wish 2BLeft totally alone. U have a longing for human contact, for the joy it brings and for the kinship it establishes. I have cousins, uncles, and aunts who are neither but the bond we share is so tight that we have a kinship that is greater than friendship. We feel like family!

Kinship is the glue that holds even the weakest of bonds together. U see other nationalities at least as members of the family, therefore certain kindnesses are extended to others on behalf of this sameness shared. Kinship with each other and the kinship we share with our Creator make us brothers and sisters. Albeit distant relatives, we respect each other enough to tolerate each other. Kinship is precious; it keeps us from destroying the human race.

Love, marriage, and friendship is kinship in motion. In your desire to preserve and strengthen the bond U have with another U upgrade the relationship from friend to partner, from partner to spouse. A new born child creates deep bonds between a couple and the two families. Marriage, marries families together, not just a man and a woman. New bonds are established and the family is extended across culture, race, and language in some cases. Kinship enriches the lives of the entire family structure if properly respected. Kinship can be tested, twisted, and tighten if U just hold on to life's lessons the journey brings. Kinship is precious and the rarest of all bonds.

Kinships help U to discover The Power 2BU! In many cases 2BU! is directly derived from the kinships in your life. U inherit more than blood from your mother and father. The family members have a first and lasting impression on your beliefs, attitudes, and enthusiasm 2BU! The places U live, worship, play, and get educated all give U the familiar faces in your life. These kinships form U; develop your sensitivities, and your worldview. Yes, each human contact is oh so rare and oh so precious that U should cherish it in the pursuit 2BU!

The Power 2BU! is a collection of rare but precious contacts. Kinship is not totally based on blood or marriage, kinships are personal choices. U choose to associate with this person or that person and each choice either gives U The Power 2BU! or it hinders U from gaining full potential. 2BNew! can be discovered by forming new bonds, new kinships, and new relationships with strangers, co-workers, and different family members who can maximize your potential instantly!

Learn 2BWise!

"We are drowning in information but starved for knowledge." -- John Naisbitt

I was just saying...

U live in an information-saturated world where everything is 24/7, 365 days a year, yet wisdom is in short supply. There are third world nations lagging behind the U.S.A. in information but surpass the U.S.A. in knowledge.

Information is useless! Who needs information for the sake of having information, except people who gossip. Knowledge is more valuable than information. Structuring information in such a fashion as to produce knowledge that is what learning is about. U have not learned anything if U are not able to produce a new set of variables from the information U have. Learning enriches your life, not information. A string of facts are lifeless until the facts aid U in deriving knowledge from them.

Learning from the cradle to the grave is the way to constantly supply U with The Power 2BU! Learn from the good and the bad times in your life. If U fail to learn then U fail 2BSucceessful. Most learning takes place in the streets not in schoolhouses. Life takes place in the back allies, on street corners, and in your home. What I mean is U put information to the test in the places U live, work and play. Schools give U vital information but U never really know how it works for

U until U take it to the places U do business. There U will discover how the information applies in your life or situations. The lessons learned give U knowledge U come to trust. Who cares about how the same information worked for John, Paul and Mary.

Learning and gaining knowledge helps shape your character and your spiritual beliefs. Your beliefs are formed while U learn from different experiences and information. The lifestyle U live is supported by your construct of the information U learn from. Knowledge, your knowledge, does not have to be the truth to work for U. It just needs 2BSomething U trust more than other versions of the same information.

Learn something every opportunity U get. Enrich your life with questions, experiences, and situations which increase your knowledge. U were created 2BWise! 2BU! takes information 2BRepackaged into knowledge, which makes U wise.

Make Mistakes!

"Mistakes are part of the dues one pays for a full life." -- Sophia Loren

I was just saying...

S uccess and failure are byproducts of the same process, pursuing The Power 2BU! Mistakes are a part of the journey. 2BU! takes twice as many mistakes as it does successes. If U want to renew, rethink and reposition your life, then be prepared to make mistakes.

Resilience begins with your first mistake. If taken right, U start learning from the setbacks in your life. Rethinking of the information U operated off of, triggering a renewal of the construct of the information. This produces better knowledge allowing U to reposition self, thereby making U a wiser person with a new perspective.

Mistakes are essential to The Power 2BU! for without mistakes U would not discover who U are or what U really want. U should cherish mistakes and the information gained. Mistakes can save your life. A detour in life may be just what U needed to arrive at the right set of variable to bring success one step closer. Never underestimate the value of a mistake. If U are really thinking U will learn more from your mistakes than U will from your successes. Remember, a stumble just may prevent a fall.

More people gain success by way of errors then any other means. U should anticipate mistakes. Going through life thinking only good is going to happen is very unwise indeed. When U anticipate U can accept missteps when they happen. Acceptance is better than sticking your head in the sand as if nothing is wrong. Don't go off the deep end and self-destruct.

Next it would do U some good if U analyze the fall out from your blunders. Thomas Edison said he had not failed 100 times but discovered 100 ways how not to make a light bulb. Each error lead to new information, he was learning all the time until he gained the knowledge to keep the light bulb lit. Then he applied that knowledge which made him wiser than others at the time about illumination. He applied what he learned to other invention. The final thing U need to do is appreciate your journey. Enjoy the mistake process. It is better known as the road to success.

U have to pay your dues just like everybody else. Mistakes are the cradle of learning. Without a few under your belt, success is not as sweet. The bitter and the sweet, the difficulty and the ease, or the ups and downs all have more value on the road 2BU! Blunders bring out the fallacy, flaws, and faults in U, your plans, and your search for answers give U The Power 2BNew!

The Power 2BU! should be the result of your mistakes. Success is not the thing that renews U; it is the slip-ups, the bloopers, and the typos that create learning opportunities for U 2BNew! Mistakes are the heart of maximizing your potential 2BU!

Nature: Your Garden of Eden!

"The richness I achieve comes from Nature, the source of my inspiration." -- Claude Monet

I was just saying...

Your nature is the part of U which benefits from enrichment. Your internal self is found in your nature. Every individual is given a personality or disposition which is the heart and soul of who they are. It is this nature, U should be most mindful of in your daily pursuit of life, liberty, and happiness. If U go against your nature, U will hear from your conscious.

Nature is the source of your inspiration. It is said, "That he who attend to his nature is inspired, but he who neglect his nature is ruined." Some call it the soul, your heart, or your personality; I call it your nature. Your world or lifestyle springs from your nature. If U are not in touch with your nature, U can build a lifestyle that is opposed to your nature which could lead to depression, low self-esteem, and the fear of success. Your conscious is the voice of your nature.

If your mistakes in life have taken U so far off course that U are unsure of self, then slow down and get in touch with your nature again. All is not lost! U can rise from the ashes of your pass. Your nature is still ready to inspire U. Nurture yourself back to good health, then discover, dream, and design a new destiny, one that inspires U 2BU! Most likely U have not done permanent damage to the essence of your

29

being, so all is not lost. The human soul is quite resilient!

Your nature is paramount and requires the utmost of attention from U. Nature gives U the first hint of who U are. If your nature is quiet then don't try to be rough, if your nature is outgoing then put yourself in a social environments which inspires that spirit in U. Some people are natural born thinkers; others like to take charge, while others are inspired by love. What inspires your nature? How do U achieve richness? These are central questions. The answers can maximize your potential instantly 2BU!

Your nature is crying out for U to turn around, slow down, and listen to it for a change. Do not think just because U have been living, thinking, and acting in a certain manner that this is U. Your present lifestyle may not agree with your nature. If U ignore your conscious too long U and it will not be on speaking terms any more. Or at least, only speak on special occasions, like divorces, rehab and funerals. Don't let it come to this!

Your potential is within U. When U discover it, U will be enthusiastic. U will achieve richness. Attend to your nature more than U attend to your clothes, money, finger nails, and hairstyle. The Power 2BU! is 2BEnthusiastic about achieving richness.

Your nature is the Garden of Eden. Cultivate the soil of your soul, take long walks among the forest of your nature, and sit for hours upon hours by the rivers that run deep in your veins. Stare endlessly into the blue sky of your spiritual being. Sleep under the moonlight and wish upon the first star U see 2BNew!

Observation: The Weak Link!

"Reason, observation, and experience; the holy trinity of science." -- Robert Green Ingersoll

I was just saying...

As U travel through life U should learn to smell the roses. Observation gives U time to see, feel, smell, and touch life on your long nature walk. If U begin to observe self in action, in the moment, U will learn things about U that will help U understand U better.

Reason, observation, and experience are the holy trinity of The Power 2BU! all working together to give U better insight into your life. Observation is usually the weak link. U are rushing here and there, doing little to no observation of your world or of self. U reason then U experience; learning from the outcome of your actions and behaviors, instead of using observation to better the outcome. U can improve your odds of success if U take time to observe before U act. Observation is information gathering, studying, or investigating to give reason what it needs to make the best decision. My father use to tell me, "When all else fail, read the instructions." Reading the instructions is observation. It gives U a better experience and your success rate goes up tenfold.

U have three tools reason, observation, and experience, but it is the middle one, observation which enrich U the most. U think reason and experience is king because U were taught that reason is the superior U and experience is the best teacher in life. This belief has U living a life of hard knocks. U learned to use observation as a last resort to gain the most from experiences. The saying, "Hindsight is 20-20" is observation as a last resort. U observe when all else fails, when U should observe before things fall apart and U have a melt down. Observation can give U 20-20 foresight. Why drive looking in the rear view mirror the whole trip.

Life gets better when U strengthen your weak link. Observation brings about The Power 2BNew! Observation allows U to stop, look, and listen before major mistakes occur. Observation fortifies reason and experience. Before all else fail, observe yourself, observe your reasoning skills, and observe your experiences. Learn to reflect, look before U leap, and read the instructions.

The question, "Who am I?" starts with observation and not reason nor experience. If anything will mess U up, it is reason and experience. Observation is a tool used to cultivate discovery, dreams, and the designs which maximize your potential 2BU!

Pilgrimage of the Soul!

"The soul passeth from form to form; and the mansions of her pilgrimage are manifold." --
Georg Hermes

I was just saying...

L ife is a journey. Life is a long walk. Life is a pilgrimage. Life is an evolution. No matter how U say it, life is movement, transitions, and transformations of one's soul 2BNew!

U should not look for a comfortable place to park self. U should find new roads and pathways to travel. U should not want to become a harden object but U should seek to stay open to the possibilities of tomorrow. Life should find U passing through many forms. Never see yourself as a finish product but as being on a long walk, in many temperatures, many lands, and meeting many faces. U have many forms of your soul which U need to discover, nurture, and observe in order 2BU!

While U may live in the same house, on the same block, and walk to the same corner market, internally U should be evolving as a person. Internally U are on a pilgrimage, a spiritual-evolution, generating the Power 2BNew! Pilgrimage is not as much a physical movement as it is a spiritual-evolution within. Reading, pondering, and questioning your philosophy, ideology, and spiritual dimensions gives U the power to reason, observe and experience the pilgrimage firsthand.

People spend large sums of money traveling to special locations on a pilgrimage to see sights, to walk where the prophets walked or to drink from wells of water but that same person will not spend two minutes to pilgrimage inside of self. What good is it to travel long distances to walk with a million strangers if U can not walk with the stranger within, right here, right now!

The greatest pilgrimage is within, not without. Life is truly enriched when U take a very personal, internal, spiritual-evolution sojourn with self. Pilgrimage to your valley floor, mountain peaks, and blue ocean of emotions, reasoning patterning, and beliefs that make U tick. Go on an expedition to explore your dreams, imaginations, and visions of U. U are transforming inside. The person U want to be is reaching out to U, crying, crying, and crying for U to take his/her hand. Don't let yourself slip back into darkness.

Take the pilgrimage serious! U do not have to pack a suitcase, buy a plane ticket, or make room reservations. U can fore go the crowds, tour guides and tour maps. Take a soulful tour, learn, and observe the spiritual evolution 2BU! up close and personal. Visit the many mansions within. Become familiar with the landscape of your garden. Get your hands dirty planting dreams and watering destiny. Take the journey of a lifetime for U will never pass this way again. U only live once, so take the scenic route home. Discover the joy, be enthusiastic, and forgive all that U meet, especially self.

Quiz Yourself!

I was just saying...

Today is a good day to quiz yourself!

A) What are my top three personal goals?

B) Why am I so committed to my top three goals?

C) What type of person must I become to achieve what I want?

D) What are my greatest fears about success?

E) What is it about me that hold me back?

F) What do I value most in my life?

G) What are my guiding principles in life?

H) What three character traits define me?

Now we are getting some where! Questions are powerful but answers can knock U off your feet. U have to ask the right questions, at the right time, to 2BU! Inquiry stimulates The Power 2BNew! process. Once U ask questions, your life is on the cusp of enrichment. When U attempt to give meaning to questions, U trigger the pilgrimage process. U learn from questions. Observation awakens questions within U.

U have to test what U believe. If U fear things that run counter to what U believe then U really need to question that which U believe. If your beliefs cannot withstand opposing views then U most likely have a plagiarized life. Your life is not real, it is borrowed, plastic. If U fear the question, than U fear success. Cheating only masks your fear.

Are U the kind of person who cheats on a quiz? It might make U feel better to get a high score but the questions are more important than the answers at this point. Who cares about the answer if U failed to learn anything 2BWise! Its questions that produce powerful discoveries 2BU!

Life is a quiz, a series of tests, proposing questions which beg answers. As the joke goes, "Don't get mad just because U don't know the answer." Plagiarizing is not the answer either. More people are living plagiarized lives today than ever before. Artificial, non-authentic lives are lived as if they are real. U are not U unless U look like a magazine picture, or the latest urban entertainer, or have someone else's name on your chest or butt. U wear large fake diamond earrings pretending, but U R just a "wanna be." U believe what the majority believe because it is safer. Plagiarized lifestyles lived as if it were your own! Where is the authentic U?

The Power 2BU! comes from heart-felt answers and a willingness to pilgrimage from mistakes to answers. Most of what U believe, U do not really believe. This is why U hate quizzes. It reveals your plagiarized, non-authentic life and all of its pain. Cross-examination leads to confusion, U feel like U are being interrogated but the truth is, questions reveal weakness in your plagiarized life.   Where is the authentic U?

Questions empower U 2BNew! Answers give U the power 2BU! Don't give padded answers, dig deep inside and ask yourself, "Is this my final answer." Is it the sum total of U or is this a borrowed answer from childhood, parents, or the streets. Due diligence is a must to maximize your potential 2BU!

Reason: It's The Why Question!

"I think the whole reason for my life is in there somewhere." -- Chaka Khan

I was just saying...

U have to discover the reason for life, your life especially. Reason gives U a reason to raise, overcome obstacles, and to stay committed. The reason should be compelling enough to ignite the fire of enthusiasm.

How strong is your reason? Do U have a reason for your reason? Do U know your why? All of this is important, why are U so committed? A reason is more than a notion to come up with when U are in the mist of wrath and mayhem. If your life is in flux it is a good time to ponder your reason. If it is not in flux, re-examine your reason to discover new options, do some fine tuning, and re-commit to the reason 2BU! Think about where U want to end up and what type of person will U need to become prior to arrival. Quiz yourself!

Start today! Define the reason U have oxygen in your lungs. Why does your existence make sense? What reason would give U an opportunity to live your life in living color? Discovery is the beginning of discovering a reason. It starts with questions that take U back to your nature to uncover your natural abilities served up with the breath of life. What are U not good at could tell U the direction not to move in. Or inform U of new skills needed 2BU! Likes and dislikes, people verses things, or crowd's verses being alone, what are your preferences?

Your reason is in there somewhere, but U might have to dream it up. U might have to design a reason. Establish goals, develop plans, or try this and that before U come face to face with your reason. Destiny is not an easy thing to stumble upon, but it is in there. Reason and destiny could be the same thing. Or U could have a new reason every five years if U wish. Reasons come and go. It is okay for the reason to evolve over time. It could start out small and grow huge or U could start huge and at the end of life be content with a very simple reason.

Just know that there is a reason in there somewhere. The Power 2BU! hinges on your reason 2BNew! The whole reason for your life is inside of U somewhere. The answer only has to make sense 2U!

How many people believed in Walt Disney's dream of a huge amusement park. Very few! Walt's reason made sense to him, he committed himself, then discovered, dreamed, and designed his destiny and voila, Disneyland was born. Ordinary people who find extraordinary reasons turn setbacks into destiny. George Washington Carver, Henry Ford, Caesar Chavez, Martin Luther King, and thousand others found The Power 2BNew! History bears witness. Why not U?

Cultivate The Seed!

"I want to cultivate the seed that was placed in me until the last small twig has grown." -- Kathe Kollwitz

I was just saying...

Your lifelong work until your dying breath, is to cultivate the seed within U. It is by way of the seed that U are enriched. In your nature is a seed which requires constant cultivation. All that U will ever be is contained In your seed and the quality of The Power 2BU! is determined by how well U cultivate it until the last small twig has grown from your being.

U do not happen by accident! Life is not fair or unfair, it is all 40 acres without a mule, awaiting cultivation of the seeds U inherited or planted. Cultivation increases the value of the land. Cultivation produces a better quality crop then untilled seeds. U can possess a special seed that few have witnessed but U will never know without cultivating your land. The seeds within U are the essence of your being. U have to create the right environment for the seed to produce to its fullness. Cultivation, preparing the soil, watering, pruning, and harvesting at the peak of ripeness are skills U have to learn if U want 2BNew!

Farmers are amazing people! They look at the land and talk to it like a man in love with a woman. They are very hands-on, very protective, and at any sign of danger, he is up all night and day attending to precious mother earth. U can learn a thing or two from a farmer. As my father said, "When we were men, we were farmers."

I have a farmer friend who planted seeds which took five years to mature before they were ready for market. Your seeds may take 5, 10, or 20 years to "pay off," but U must never stop tilling the land, attending to the seeds, and caring for the crops. Every seed is not seasonal. Short term gains are not always wise. Avoid "get rich quick" seeds. Long term growth seeds produce a more resilient U. Life wants to produce every twig it is capable of pushing forth. U should want to see your entire 40 acres in full bloom, heavy with fruit, with deep roots, rivers flowing, and huge mansions.

Cultivation reveals the natural minerals in the soil – natural gas, gold, oil, coal, and diamonds. The list is endless as to what the breath of life deposited within U. When is the last time U walked your land? Dug deep into the soil? Removed the boulders and dry brush? If U fail to cultivate, your land will always only be worth minimum wage.

If U choose to use chemicals, i.e. drugs or other intoxicants, your land may be forever contaminated. The HazMat Team may be needed to decontaminate your land. More farmers are using organic, old-school, cultivation methods nowadays. More consumers are demanding organic grown foods. Take a hint!

Seeds are also akin to ideas, thoughts, or dreams. They all need cultivation to survive. Education and learning is a tool of cultivation. U are 40 acres without a mule! It is your responsibility to build your life out until the last twig appears on the tree. U have one lifetime to do it, just like every one else. Remember life is time sensitive!

Your land is just as valuable as the next person. The difference is the other man or woman knows they have a seed within them, and the best way to know what kind of seed it is, is to cultivate their life, their land, which require getting their hands dirty. The Power 2BU! is dirty work!

Therapy Benefits U!

"Therapy can help U grow. Fears will just disappear." -- Stephanie Mills

I was just saying...

Look at therapy as seeking correction, solutions or restoration. Therapy can become a power tool in the battle 2BU! U do not have to be 51-50 to need therapy. Normal people need therapy 2BNew!

U can gain a lot of mileage out of therapy in your present state. The goal of therapy is to smooth U out 2BU! It is like recreation renews and revitalizes U. A vacation can be therapy or a day without your spouse and the children. Therapy may take the form of 18 holes of golf, or a day with the grandchildren or a long walk to no place special.

2BU! is therapeutic. It heals, soothes, and cures things before they get out of hand and U need real help. Few things can help U if U wait too late before U seek to solve your issues. Therapy can be a very spiritual experience. It heals the soul, mind, and body. It is a form of cultivation, pampering of the soul. It can reveal hidden treasures beneath your land. U should not be a stranger to therapy. It is not all about laying on a couch being quizzed about your childhood, parents, or your nightmares. Therapy is clearing your land of boulders, stumps, and fallen tree branches.

Look at all of the medicine taken by children for depression, hyperactive behavior, and ADHD. Where did all of this break down come from, lack of therapy. Parenting is therapy, father-daughter talks, mother-son talks, family meetings, and everyone around the dinner table is therapy. Kinships are an important part of therapy. U need a friend U can think out loud with, share humor with, and enjoy the journey with.

Build a little therapy into your life. If U need real help don't be ashamed to get it. In the meantime, slow your roll; take a little "me" time; some time to find a reason, to water the seeds, and to forgive 2BU! Get committed, develop a positive attitude, and learn from your mistakes. Therapy can help U refine and define your destiny, give U better observation tools, and confirm your beliefs. Never underestimate The Power 2BU! therapy sessions.

Therapy is not all business and no play. Recreation is re-creation. It is recommended that U hit play, and play hard and long, as often as U can. Turn the music up loud and dance 'till your legs give out. Yes, pencil in playtime into your busy schedule. Have fun, avoid risky behavior. Look for opportunities to enjoy the joy day or night. Fun, real fun, can erase years of pain. Look for opportunities 2BRenewed, and 2BLoved by U. Therapy is enriching!

Therapy should not be a taboo subject. U need to re-boot your hard drive 2BU! re-create 2BNew!, re-store 2BU!, re-cultivate 2BNew!, and re-generate 2BU! Therapy is about heart-to-heart talks, journaling, reading, swimming, loving, or whatever re-charges your batteries 2BU! Therapy benefits U!

Utter Health-Felt-Truth!

"Poetry is the utterance of deep and heart-felt truth - the true poet is very near the oracle." --
Edwin Hubbel Chapin

I was just saying...

A very powerful therapy is to utter heart-felt-truth. When U learn not to suffer in silence and speak heart-felt-truth U will feel The Power 2BU! Let the world know who U are, what U think, and what U want. Weigh in above the two cents level. Go for the whole enchilada without shame or blame.

Utterance is not offending, hurting, or cursing others. It is finding your voice! A voice of truth which echoes your authentic heart-felt-truth that springs from your nature, your seed, and your beliefs. The real U finally speaks from years of observation, kinships, and commitments which define U. Finding one's voice is a pilgrimage from learning 2BWise! The truth is that the majority of people fail to find their heart-felt-truth. Others are 40 and older before they begin to utter a word of truth.

Utterance is not reserved for the rich and famous, or the bold and restless, or the insane. U have the right to voice your opinion, express yourself in poetry, song, or rap. Why not write a book, a novel or an autobiography. Develop a screenplay. Tell your story on the silver screen.

It is time U deliver to the world your philosophy, ideology, and theology.   Make statements that represent the seeds of your nature. Make remarks on topics that U are passionate about. March in protest of things that U feel strongly about. Call into your favorite talk show to let them know U have an opinion that is well thought out. Don't just mouth off or ramble, but speak with eloquence like U have a PhD on the topic at hand being the wise person U are.

Articulation is important! U need to be able to tell your story. Give your life power and meaning when U inform others of the rare and precious kinships from the many places, spaces, and faces U have encountered in your life. Despite the hardships, tell your story with a positive attitude. Hearing your story will renew your enthusiasm. Utterance leads to The Power 2BU! Getting up in front of people to speak empowers U to raise your expertise status. U gain influence when U utter heart-felt-truths. U can become an expert to millions. Why let Dr. Phil, Bill O'Reilly, or The View crew have the last word.

Practice utterance to the utmost! Empower yourself to speak, to rise your hand in disagreement or agreement or to utter words of love for people, places, and things U feel so passionately about. Words make U! Words spoken, written, sung, and rapped all are the makings of U! Never underestimate your heart-felt-truth because it just might be the utterance of encouragement a child needs to hear at that very moment 2BNew!

The Veracity 2BU!

"**We appreciate frankness from those who like us. Frankness from others is called insolence.**" -- Andre Maurois

I was just saying...

Candor, frankness, or veracity can go a long ways to improve your mental, spiritual, and emotional state.

As much as U resist being honest on sensitive topics, it can clear your soul and give U room to breath once U are. This is not in support of people who "speak" their mind and say, "Oh well! Just had to get that off my chest." This is about truthfulness that really helps, not harm. Veracity is a real attempt at being upright, straightforward, and honest.

Veracity enriches the listener and the speaker. When U are sincere, people respect where U are coming from. U gain certain reliability even though they disagree with U. It is hard sometimes to be honest in situations U suspect your words will cause pain or hurt. These circumstances call for tact, diplomacy, and veracity. Normally, in the end everyone is enriched by the conversation. It is therapeutic, like a good foot massage.

One of the hardest spaces to practice veracity is when emotions are high and the stakes are even higher. Being an emotional coward is a real fact of life. U want to shrink and disappear at times but 2BU! at moments like this is vital to your development. U feel threaten; ugly words are thrown at U. Take a moment, step back, if it is safe, then speak heart-felt-truth. Make sure the other person is not moving from silence to violence.

The Power 2BU! is not ease. There are tough choices to be made. The U today may not be the same U who appears tomorrow. Then there are days that being U is the last thing on your mind. 2BU! is the hardest thing U will do in your entire life. Everything else is a cake walk in comparison. Veracity is what U have to be with yourself everyday. Be honest with U, even when U lie to others. Have a frank conversation with your spirit while U are making excuses for your laziness. Do not let yourself off of the hook for cheating. Don't mask over your fears, speak up and be real about what U have to do the next time fear raises its voice to silence U.

Practice veracity on your own land; speak to your seed to help it break through tough ground. Utter words of veracity to yourself in hard times, bad times, and low self-esteem times. Veracity can help build and fortify a positive attitude. Frankness is good for the soul, your soul. It takes all of your energy 2BNew! Veracity can help energize U 2BU!

What Do U Want!

"After you get what you want you don't want it."
-- Irving Berlin

I was just saying...

The central question in life enrichment is, "What do U really, really want?" Put another way, "If U knew U would die today, what will the dash, on your tombstone, between your sunrise and sunset represent?" How would others have benefited from your existence? Just being clear about what U want is enthusiastic enough 2BU! Too many people don't want what they say they want. Getting what U ask for may lead to immediate dissatisfaction.

U can work all of your life for things that matter not. Remember comfort and luxuries are not the chief requirements of life. U need to discover something 2BEnthusiastic about. What U want should make U significant. The dash needs to remind people how significant U were, not how big your house was, or the model car U drove, but the seed from which U sprung, the richness of your land, and the positive attitude U spread.

As the old saying goes, "Be careful what U wish for U just might get it." U think U really want something but when its reality is shown to U, then U reject it. U claim it was not "exactly" what U asked for. Albeit, U asked for it, if not prayed for it.

What U really, really want has 2BDiscovered. It is hard work pushing below the surface to come face to face with your real dreams. What do U honestly desire, crave, or hunger for at the heart of U! U can emotionally need one thing which is totally opposite of what U want. U need one thing but U want another. Want is a personal choice. What U want speaks to the core of U, your hopes and dreams 2BU!

Knowing your wants empowers U to plan your path. It helps direct your attitude away from negative thoughts. It gives U something to focus on. It will produce a spirit of commitment to continue to cultivate self into the person U need to be in order to achieve The Power 2BNew! Want gives U resilience to endure and to get up when U fall. If U misidentify what U want, U could end up with all that U wanted but dissatisfied and depressed.

Want is what U work for, wake up for, and wonder about more than sex. What are U willing to sacrifice for, stay committed to, and 2BNew! to achieve? What is so lacking in U that it leaves a hole in your existence? What do U really, really want for U? It is okay to be a little selfish, because it is personal. Your pursuit of it will give U The Power 2BU! It will change your behavior, values, and principles 2BNew!

The dash on your tombstone is what it all comes down to. What will it tell people about your ability to master The Power 2BU!

XXX Threat!

"2BU! is an extemporaneous expressive extol which will exhilarate U2BNew! 2BNew! is an extraordinary exuberant exigency exchange 2BU!" -- Thomas Abdul-Salaam

I was just expressing...

The XXX threat is the pursuit of excellence with exceptional excitement. Exert yourself 2BU! It is an exercise that U must not exempt self from. Your existence is an expedition to expel all that is not U from U.

The most expensive expenditure will be your exchange in the fight for the explicit right 2BU! To expand your explanation, to explain, and expiate 2BNew! Life is not an experiment extended to U. It is an extreme extrication 2BU! What is in your seed that needs to exude to the surface until U come eyeball 2 eyeball with U.

U R the executive of your life. U R in charge of all extenuating circumstances in your life. U have to extinguish the fires in your life. U have to exult yourself. U have to excel. U cannot make exception for your behavior. U have to be an example. U can examine your actions, behaviors, and beliefs. U cannot exempt U from the exercise 2BU! Choose 2BExcited 2BU! U have to go to excruciating pain 2BNew! U have to exploit yourself...before everyone else use U for their exploitation. U have to expunge the old U for the new U.

U R a full fledged legal "person" accountable for all actions, decisions, expenditures, exchanges, and the profits and losses in your life. U R the CEO, head honcho of the original business, LIFE, YOUR LIFE. Adam and Eve both executed their executive rights 2BFruitful! and Multiply! Exhaustion is part of the pursuit 2BU! Life is an excretion, life is an expedition! U should become an expert on what it takes 2BU!

Life can be an extemporaneous act. Ad-libbing is required at times. Your exterior may not be the best expression of U, therefore get to know the interior U even betterl. Learn its heart-felt-truth. Always be exhilarated about the possibilities 2BNew!   U R extraordinary! There is an exigency 2BU!

I shall exit with these departing words, U R an exquisite external expression exulted 2B an exuberant extension of the Exalted God!

Yearn 2BU!

"Life is a series of collisions with the future; it is not the sum of what we have been, but what we yearn to be." -- Jose Ortega y Gasset

I was just saying...

Of all of your wants, at some point in time U should have as your greatest want, the yearn 2BU! on a grand scale. Not, Donald Trump grand, but as in Grand Canyon. People will journey long distances just to stand in your presence, to marvel at your natural talents, and the depth of your soul. That kind of grand!

Yearning 2BU! is a series of mistakes, accidents, and collisions with your future. How do U think the Canyon became the "Grand" Canyon. It was formed over thousands; some say millions, of years of collisions, upheavals, and adversities to create a one-of-a-kind wonder. U are on your way to being a one-of-a-kind wonder, if U will just endure the collisions in your life. Maintain the yearning 2BGrand in the most marvelous way U can imagine.

Never marvel at someone else's life to the point that U yearn 2BThem. Michael Jordan is great but U don't want 2BLike Mike, U want to be as grand but U! Don't be so star struck of others, see yourself being the star on the red carpet of your life, unique and Grand Canyon kind of wonderful. Never want, desire, or yearn 2BOther than the person U keep colliding into.

Get to know that person who calls out to U, yearning 2BNew!

Everyday yearn 2BU!   Yearn to know U! Be who U want to be! Push on U, pull on U, and occasionally yell at U, in a polite way, 2BU!   U should want to rise above the television version of U, the super model U or the American Idol star struck U. Want to hear what U yearn 2B! Not the plastic, non-authentic U! But the "U get what U see" U! Pray everyday 4U! Write with the wish and hope that your utterance keeps the yearning in U 2BU! alive and well.

The Power 2BU! enriches U to become GRAND as the Grand Canyon kind of wonderful!

The End Zone!

"If U put yourself in a position where U have to stretch outside your comfort zone, then U are forced to expand your consciousness." -- Les Brown

I was just saying...

Being comfortable is not a bad thing, it's just not a good thing in the pursuit 2BNew! Comfortable can lure U into a false sense of security. The zone U want to be in is inquiry, discovery, and experimentation with the Power 2BU!

Comfort zones tend to give other people control over U. U feel too safe and satisfied. In the military we had a saying, "Fat, dumb and happy." That's a real definition of comfort zone. Again, not a bad thing, just not a good thing if U are serious about the journey 2BU!

There are normally four zones, or cycles, U pass though on your journey 2BU! On any given day U could be in one or more zones. They are Comfort, Fear, Inquiry, and Commitment. The comfort zone is where U spent most of your life. U like being comfortable because U are happy, everything is fine, and U can normally predict the next move, if U have to think about it at all. Comfort is good, but not if U want what U want. U have to reach, stretch, and think outside your comfort zone if U want what U want.

The zone that keeps U in comfort is fear. U become nerves when U think outside of your comfort zone.

Self-doubt, anxiety, and anger could be some of the things U feel. U become unsure of self from the challenge of finding new ground. U ask yourself, "Why move when things are so great right here, right now!" Fear pushes answers back and builds excuses for why the comfort zone is so comfortable. But if U can wade your way through the jungle of fear and resistance The Power 2BU! will have U quizzing self.

Inquiry can save the day. To quiz oneself is a very powerful act. Never be afraid of the questions nor the answers U produce, or the fear of not knowing. It is questions that enrich the soil of your being. Questions lead to discovery of new boundaries, frontiers, and The Power 2BNew! Old school works but new school can be more exciting. All that U experience today, in the form of technology, is because as Hewlett-Packard said "We asked the 'What if...' question." Are U afraid of the what if question? If U don't ask it some one will and they will be as grand as the Grand Canyon and U will be marveling at them wondering, "How did she become so grand?"

Then there is the Commitment zone. This is the zone where the real work takes place. Once U are committed 2BU! then U empower yourself 2BNew! U will know when U are there; because U can't sleep, you're too busy taking action. U take risk but you're not risky. U study information and learn 2BWise! Commitment energizes U, gives U the positive attitude needed to live outside of your comfort zone.

Eventually U will find self back in the comfort zone, don't worry! Just ask the what if... question and it will catapult U over the fear zone into the land of Inquiry, the land of enrichment, the end zone!

Conclusion: Don't Stop Thinking!

A conclusion is the place where you get tried of thinking. — Martin Henry Fischer

I was just saying...

Life enrichment is a state of being, a series of questions, positive responses, and a foundation of principles, behaviors, and actions. It is not a conclusion! Life enrichment is not a search for the end of things, but discovery of new talents, options, and roads to travel.

Cycles help U see farther than conclusions. Life enrichment is not a dead end road. It is a vista! From where U stand today it may look like the road ends but it goes on forever. All U have to do is be brave enough to take the journey. U will be a better person for it.

When the world was flat, man was afraid to go too far away from home for fear he would far of the edge. There was little learning. Man had a lot of information but he was unable to turn it into knowledge. He was unaware that he was on a ball spinning nearly 25,000 miles per hour. When U see conclusions U get tried of thinking.

Life was enriched with the discovery that the earth was circular, it brought about new discoveries. When man realized that things went around and around, there were no end in sight, his thinking improved 10 fold. Your vision and thinking is connected. Your thinking is limited by your vision. If U see the road as a dead end, your thinking will lead to dead ends. Life enrichment is a cycle of discoveries, dreams, and designs. Just because U are down today, know this too will pass. Life is not an 90 degree angel nor an 180 degree angel, it is 360 degrees, circular process.

Comfort zones come and go, but never stop asking questions, discovering, dreaming, and designing. Destiny is not the end of life; it is the purpose of life. Discovering your destiny will enrich life's journey.

Enrichment is passing from form to form, seeking to live a quality, authentic life. It is enduring the journey until your Lord calls U home. As a song put it, "If I should wake up and find that the world has turned to stone and my Lord said it is time to come home, I will be satisfied that I had loved U." The life was enriched by the giving and receiving love. How would U know U had lived a quality life?

The ABC's of Life Enrichment are 27 tools assembled in one tool box, The Power 2BU! gift pack. It is not a step-by-step guide to self-improvement. It is your travel kit as U journey from form to form. Keep it in the glove box or your briefcase, or on the seat beside U.

What will the dash represent between your sunrise and sunset? What meaning did U derive from life? What did U give to others? R U a Johnny Appleseed, spreading joy or a Johnny come lately, a taker, always counting your money at the table, worried about winning and losing?

Conclusions are good for books but not Life Enrichment. The Power 2BU! is a constant making good, better. Enrich self as often as humanly possible.

The Power 2BU! wants U to never say never to your dreams, regardless of your present-day state of affairs, circumstances, or financial status. Dreams are real! As Tupac put it, "Reality lied! Dreams are real!" If U give up, your dreams die. U don't want that! Believe in the "God within" all the days of your life! Live your authentic lifestyle, from this day forward!

It's a great day 2BU!

Thomas Abdul-Salaam
Twin Servant of Peace

18 Bonus Tips!
My Gift 2U!
(Thank U for supporting this book.)

Bonus Table of Contents

Dreams R Real!

"Nothing is as real as a dream. The world can change around you, but your dream will not. Responsibilities need not erase it. Duties need not obscure it. Because the dream is within you, no one can take it away." -- Tom Clancy

I was just saying...

A dream is a promise. It is your description of a life to come. It is real the day U envision it, yet it is a promise unfulfilled. U must promise that U will work as hard as U can to achieve it. U must take full ownership of your dreams regardless of how dim it may appear to U today. Own it!

Hard times, lack of money, or set backs should not erase your desire to achieve it. The long work days, neither sleepless nights, nor the nay-sayers should be an excuse for U to disconnect with your reality. Dreams R Real!

Present-day circumstances or situations should not deflate your commitment to live the dream. Reality of today was a dream yesterday. Someone dreamed of an iPod, a Wii, and Blue tooth technology long before they were real enough to hold in your hand. Reality starts with a dream!

If U believe then it is real! If U stay committed it will be real! Your dreams are as real as U make them. The world changed because someone dreamed of how to change it, then they fulfilled the promise made to themselves. What promises have U made 2U?

The law of nature has one constant, cause and effect. Dreams are the cause and reality is the effect. The impact of a dream can be heard all around the world. Dreams thunder in the head of humans loud enough to shock one into action. Dreams produce lightening in the hearts of humans electrifying their imagination. Dreams R Powerful!

If U fail to dream, U fail to live. The nuclear energy of life is dreams. If U are bored, it is because U do not have a dream to live out. U have not promised U anything worth living for. Enthusiasm, the "God within" depends on dreams to awaken it, to fuel it, and to guide it. Oh, where, oh where have your dreams gone!

Discover your dream and U will know your purpose. The Power 2BU! starts with a dream. It starts with a promise 2BU! How will U every be U if U fail to dream, make promises, and design your reality. Destiny is a dream fulfilled! If U have nothing to fulfill, nothing that drives U, even if U lived a thousand years, enrichment would have passed U by.

Just because it did not happen last year, does not cancel it out for this year. Aim High, believe in yourself, and stand by your dreams. You have to start today to get your year in gear! Where do U want be a year from here? Start by taking a long, hard look at the dreamer, U. The central figure in your future is and will always be U. If U do not perform in a big way, big things will never happen.

Before U define the dream or write an action plan, spend some private time with your spirit, your heart, and your values. Find out how committed U are to the dream. Do U have the resilience to go the distance.

U are essential, and the better U know U, it increases your chances of success tenfold. When U learn your strengths and weaknesses, then U can align self. U know what U R working with. Know matter what happens U must continue to believe in self and your dreams. If U stop believing, the dream will cease to exist.

Dreams come from inside of U; therefore, you must be in touch with the dreamer to truly understand the dream. It is U that give the dream meaning, purpose, and direction. I am not talking about night dreams, I'm asking U, "What do U daydream about?" Dream dreams which do not require a palm reading session to have the courage to pursue. Your daydreams R revelations just as well as your night dreams!

All success begins with a dream. All dreams are a promise unfulfilled. The only question is R U a promise keeper?

Who R U!

"We must be trying to learn who we really are, rather than trying to tell ourselves who we should be." -- John Powell, S.J.

I was just saying...

Who R U? is the central question. The more U ask, the more U will discover. The question is not asking, are U a lawyer, doctor, or singer. It is asking U what do U value, what are your principles, and what is your character. Who R U defines the root or core of U.

What career path U R on is not central to this question. How big your house is or what side of town U live on is not central to this question. Who U R married to, what your children do for a living, or how fat your bank account has nothing to do with this question.

If all U have has been gotten by hook and crook, tells more about your values. Now that is central to this question. Values define U! If U justify your actions by, "It is a dog eat dog world" now that is central to this question. If U think, 'he who has the gold makes the rules' that is central to this question.

Who U R is discovered during defining moments; which reveal flaws, cracks and the person behind the mask. U may do things that run counter to your character, values or principles but U still have to get back up and met the next challenge. The answer to the question is found in those things which represent the core of U. To know thy self is a commandment, a divine decree.

It is not about telling self who U want to be, but discovering who U R. It may take a life time but the journey is worth every step. Life is better when U become U and stop living out some plastic, non-authentic version of U.

Stop and listen to your heart. Listen to your longings and the moments of joy. Where do your natural talents lead U. Learn, discover, and educate yourself about U through reflection, meditation, and dreams of a better life.

All of this leads to principles, like faith, prayer, and love for thy brother. Principles are the foundation upon which your life rest. It is the rock solid things about U that regardless of which way the wind blows, U will always be found valuing these traits. When all else fail U will still pray, fast, and pilgrimage to know U.

Character is the face of U. It is the person people meet at the water cooler, on the street, and in business meetings. U leave what I call your DNA fingerprint behind. How people think of U, interact with U and speak of U when U are not present. Do character traits like respect, honesty, and responsibility come to mind when they speak of U.

Who U R is derived from your principles, values, and your character traits. All else is a superficial U, non-authentic U! Discovering who U R is your heavenly purpose; 2BU! is your earthly mission.

Marvel @ U!

"People travel to wonder at the height of mountains, at the huge waves of the sea, at the long courses of rivers, at the vast compass of the ocean, at the circular motion of the stars, and they pass by themselves without wondering." -- Saint Augustine

I was just saying...

There is no greater wonder, no greater gift then to know thy self! Creation has given to the human being the ability to discover, dream and design its destiny. If that is not something to marvel at, then what is?

U may think the deep blue sea is amazing while U walk its shores, but have U ever walked your shoreline, swim in your ocean of possibilities, or collected the sea shells along your beach? Why not?

God's creation is a wonder to explore but God's greatest creation is U! God crowned creation with U! He signed His everlasting name when He created the human being in His image. U want something to wonder about, and then wonder about U. U R the marvel of creation.

As humans we are the only creatures capable of exploration of its own thoughts, behaviors and beliefs. Yet, U spend little to no time wondering about self. U R afraid to be in the same room with U, for fear U might start to think about U. People see it as a painful experience to spend time with their own thoughts, inner emotions or their pass, not to mention planning their future.

Before you go to bed tonight, ask yourself the why question. Why questions tend to drive you inside. The more you ask why, the deeper it will take you into your world of self discovery. Ask, "Why am I...?" "Why don't I...?" "Why do I believe...?"

Stop passing by the wonderment of your human worth. Stop star gazing and start soul searching. Find the marvelous things about U worth getting excited about. How deep is your ocean of knowledge? How tall is your mountain of talent? Follow the pathways of the rivers of your soul.

U brave shark attacks, the cold frigid waters, and the possibility of drowning, to explore the seven seas but U will not swim in the seven seas of your soul; when life dishes out similar dangers U turn to drugs, partying, and hiding under the covers. Dare to explore your seven seas! Surf your waves! Scrub dive 2Marvel U!

U R a piece of work...a divine piece of work. Marvel at that!

Impossible Situations!

"We are all faced with a series of opportunities brilliantly disguised as impossible situations." --
Chuck Swindoll

I was just saying...

A hundred years ago, the U.S. Patent Office declared, everything that could be invented had been invented. The thought was that nothing else was possible nor needed. Today, the impossible is being made possible every other day.

Humans have been doing the impossible since the first day they opened their eyes. This is the purpose of human beings. It is your mission, if U accept it. U R here to take impossible situations presented 2U and make them possible. U might know it better as, "when served lemons, make lemonade."

Impossible situations should inspire U. It should cause dreams to be born. Marvel at self, U are the impossible situation in creation. How did U come about? Why R U the only creature endowed with such intelligence, if Darwinism is right, there should still be more creatures like U walking out of the wild. U R the impossible dream! A divine decree!

U have been given the divine gift of managing impossible situations. It is not a gift given to the few, it is a gift given to the many. It is not a white thing or a black thing; it is not a color thing at all. It is a human thing! If U count yourself among that group, then U R divinely gifted to manage the impossible.

U R faced with a series of opportunities disguised as impossible situations. Everyone is faced with their own impossible situation. How U manage yours is the difference between U and the other person. God has a way of ensuring the rich face their impossible situations as well as the poor. No one escapes this test!

Opportunity is a slippery fellow. He can come suited down, looking out of your league, or in work clothes, appearing too much work and not worth it. Don't be fooled by his tricks and smooth talk. His job is to test your awareness of the gift within. If U pass on the challenge, then he wins. U lose! U turn bitter, depressed, and feel like U never got your break, but U failed to meet the impossible situation when presented 2U.

2BU! is a series of opportunities brilliantly disguised as impossible situations.

What's The Purpose!

"The basic purpose of all human activity is the protection, maintenance, and the enhancement, not of the self, but of the self-concept of self." --
Samuel I. Hayakuwa

I was just saying...

U hear all the time, peer pressure caused someone to drink or do drugs, or some other crazy thing. The real issue is the unwillingness of self to provide protection, maintenance, and enhancement of the self-concept of self.

At some point in life U have to decide who U R and be that person. This is life enrichment at its very fundamental level. It is near impossible to have a quality life if U R always subject to suggestions from others. It is also a sign of weak values, principles, and character flaws.

Your self-concept is U personified. It is the projection of the principles, values, and character traits U perceive best represent U. If U had a paint brush in your hand, how would U paint U for the world to see. Would the colors be dark, gray, and lifeless or would they be bright, warm and full of life.

When U look in the mirror who or what do U see, feel, and think about U? What are your passions? Dreams? Desires? If U were in charge of your life, who would U aspired 2B, do, and act. What principles, values, and character traits really matter 2U? How would U want to be remembered?

If U protect this person from harm, s/he will serve U well. If U drink to fit in, then U just might be compromising your self-concept of self. What's the purpose of living a whole life which contradicts your image of U. This could lead to some serious mental and spiritual problems over time.

The Power 2BU! Involves the protection, maintenance, and enrichment of the IMAGE U have or the PERSON U wish 2B! It is hard to find your purpose if U fail to imagine a self-concept of self. It's the old age question, Who R U? 2BU! U needs to understand your self-concept of self.

Goals Make It Realistic!

"Goals give you the specific direction to take to make your dreams come true." -- John Condry

I was just saying...

While dreams are real, goals make it realistic! Without goals all U have is a pipe dream.

Dreams are vague concepts of what U desire. Goals are the stepping stones that lead U to what U want. Whether U call it mission, vision, strategy, objectives, or task all are a different shade of a goal.

What is a goal? There are five components which make a goal complete. It has to be specific, measurable, achievable, realistic, and time oriented (SMART). To make it specific, U need to say exactly what U want and stop being vague. If U want to earn a degree, then say in what field of study will U engage in, what degree do wish to achieve, BA, BS, Masters, or PhD.

Measurable has to do with how will U or others know movement has taken place. U might say U will take five classes per semester, study three hour a night, and earn a 3.0 per semester. Measurable items hold your feet to the fire. If your employer where paying for U to go to school, she would be impressed by the above and be more willing to support U. Both of U would be able to know quickly if movement had taken place.

U have to determine whether a PhD is achievable. Do U understand the course work required, do U have the time, and the determination to go all the way. What can U do right now!

What is realistic for U today. If U R unable to get financial aide, maybe one class is all U should take this semester. If a car is needed to take early or late classes and U have to catch the bus then it is not realistic to sign for these classes. Do what is reasonable for U to do. If U set the bar too high, failure and disappointment will shoot a hole in your dreams. Take it slow!

Time is always a question. How much time will it take to graduate? To study? To write papers? Time will affect every aspect of your dream. The wrong approach is to use time as a reason not to achieve your dreams. Do U want it? R U committed? R U determined? If so, then U will find the time. U will give up something just to keep the dream alive.

If U apply all five components of goal setting, it will turn U in a very specific direction. The only way U will find yourself out to sea without a rudder, is if U lose sight of your goals. If U fail to be specific, to set measurable bench marks, the dream will be unachievable. If U cannot achieve it, then it is unrealistic to pursuit it. Therefore who cares how much time U have on your hands.

A person without goals is afraid of success. U don't want what U say U want. It is just that simple! 2BU! Require goals!

Creativity!

**"Creativity involves taking what you have,
where you are, and getting the most out of it."** --
Carl Mays

I was just saying...

My mother told me more than once, "Don't cry over spilled milk." Wishing the circumstances were different or had not happen is not a good use of your brain cells. U will be better served being creative about the situations.

Creativity is held back as long as U refuse to take what U have and use it to get what U want. Reality tells us that circumstance do not change without interference. Creative thinking is interference.

Here is a question I ask often, "How many ways are there to make change for a dollar?" Then I ask everyone to write out each way to make change for a dollar. This process starts the creative juices flowing.

To get from here to there requires creative problem-solving, decision-making, and options. Some call it thinking outside the box or coloring outside the lines. I like Spock's answer best from a Star Trek episode. Captain Kirk asked Spock what prompted him to take the action he did, which saved their lives, to which Spock answered, "When all logical responses fail, the most logical thing was to do the illogical." Now that is being creative!

If who U R today is not working for U or U need some fine tuning and the logical thinking is not yielding the results, then do the illogical. Apply creativity!

When U use creativity; U produce better results and more options. Once U get use to your creative powers, U will be more prolific in the number of options open 2U. It leads to a fertile brain of ideas giving U original thoughts which can really be powerful in your efforts 2BU!

Imagination is another byproduct of creativity at work. U begin to imagine new images of the future and ways to get there. Now U are on the verge of inventing, discovering and designing a destiny that is uniquely yours.

Prove Yourself!

"The difference between desire and drive is the difference between expressing yourself and proving yourself." -- Larry Wilson

I was just saying...

Many people have desire but are short on drive. The action U take is more important than all activities U do. U could be working hard but getting no where. Do the term 'spinning your wheels' come to mine when U think about your life. Most people are involved in activity and calling it action. They think they got a lot done today.

Goals are action step toward an end. Get a college degree is the end. U have to measure all of your activity for the day or week and decide how all of that moved U closer to your stated goal. If the answer is yes, then U have desire and drive. If not, then all U have is desire. Not bad, at least U R half way there.

Desire can leave U standing in the same spot, wishing and hoping. This is how life passes U by on more than one occasion. U have to learn how to drive your dreams home. Remember, in basketball it is the drive to the basket that separates the ordinary players from the Michael Jordan's of the game.

U may only have the desire to do big things but if U question self it can help develop the drive U need. Stop expressing your desires, commit to drive all the way to the basket and dunk the ball. Desire and drive need to be aligned with each other.

U have to prove yourself. Proving yourself will improve your self-esteem and your self-concept of self.

Turn desire into proof. Prove that U have the drive to play on "center court." Prove that U have the Power 2BU! Put up or shut up. Nowadays it is said, "It's time to pony up!"

Out Do U!

"Excellence demands that you be better than yourself." -- Ted Engstrom

I was just saying...

In order to grow, you must be in pursuit of something bigger than yourself. If what you're in pursuit of is small, you will be small. Big pursuits demand that you show up in a big way. The pursuit of excellence requires that U out do U!

Excellence, like success, is not a destination, but a journey. It is not perfection, or not making mistakes, or slipping a few times. It is doing better than U did yesterday or the last time U attempted the same thing. Just out perform U! Forget about Bill Gates, Donald Trump or Oprah, they have to out do themselves to maintain their level of excellence. U do not want their challenges. Concentrate on U pushing U beyond yesterday.

If U can get this stage of the game down packed, U could be the next big thing. People who become successful are the ones who out do themselves day after day, month after month, and year after year. When U get to the top, ask Oprah how she got there and she will quote these words I am speaking 2U. "I out did myself day after day."

There are no secrets to success, only people paddling the truth as a secret. Excellence is one of the longest journeys U will ever take in your life. The more U do today, only leads to longer hours tomorrow, if U take excellence serious.

On the journey to excellence, take time to reflect on what U learned, discovered and experienced. Ask positive questions concerning your new insights, beliefs, and relationships forged. Think about the new U that is emerging. Stay in touch with your emotions, esteem, and values U formed along the way.

Out doing yourself will become a habit over time. Eventually your habit of forming and meeting your goals will be second nature. U will track your progress daily and know exactly what U have to do when U awaken and what resources are needed to achieve. Time will be your friend because U manage time instead of killing time.

Excellence do not just rise out of the best of times, it can come out of the worst of times. Bad times require your performance level to peak above normal. U have more on the line in these times. Failure is not an option! It is time to find out how bad U want to succeed. Just out do U over and over and over. The next time U look up, excellence will be close at hand and The Power 2BU! will be staring U in the face.

Get the Door!

"Too often, when opportunity knocks, but by the time you push back the chain, push back the bolt, unhook the two locks, and shut off the burglar alarms, it's too late." -- Rita Coolidge

I was just saying...

Opportunity is not hard to find. With all of the pop-ups, multi-level marketing, work from home, get rich peddlers knocking, it is no wonder U have bolted the door. The problem is U have not seen a real, honest opportunity in months, if not years.

A real opportunity is favorable to your present-day circumstances. If U have been trying to go to school, an opportunity should move U closer to that goal. What U have become accustom to is called "opportunism." This approach requires U to shift in its direction, albeit a direction that moves U away from your goals. U never intended to be a Fuller Brush salesperson, but because "there is big money to be made" U shift directions. Now U are an Opportunist.

After chasing 10 or 20 of these "secret" ways or methods, U R still no closer to your masters' degree. More and more doors are being bolted shut due to opportunism.

Here is a few clues:

→ If it is too good to be true, then it is not for U!

→ If U can sit around in your pajamas all day, that is opportunism.

→ If the product or services sells itself and it is not money, then that's opportunism, bypass on it.

Here is when it might be wise to get the door:

→ It invites U to something that is already a natural fit.

→ It actually moves U toward your stated goals.

→ It is a risk but it is not a risky investment or act.

→ It does not require U do go against your values.

U have to evaluate every opportunity and don't be so eager that U become opportunistic. If this is the sign hanging on your door, there will be plenty of knocks but very few opportunities.

Opportunity involves work, not slick marketing schemes. If U are not willing to work hard, then stop answering the door. If "secrets" interest U, then be prepared 2BTaken to the cleaners over and over again.

U-R-A Leader!

"The role of a leader is to enhance, transform, coach, care, trust, and cheerlead. The activities of the leader are to educate, sponsor, coach, and counsel using appropriate timing, tone, consequences, and skills." -- Tom Peters and Nancy Austin, Passion for Excellence

I was just saying...

Understand this; know matter what your position or title, U R A leader. First and foremost, U-R-A leader of your life. Everyday U must lead, direct, and act in order for U to have the lifestyle U want. Leadership is a must, 24/7!

Your role is to enhance your life. Enrichment enhances life. Growth, development, education, all enhances life. Transforming self is your leadership role. It is important that you learn to coach yourself. Establish practice times, develop drills, and create a game plan for the big game.

Trust U with the ball with 2.5 second remaining. If U do not trust self in tough situations who are U going to trust? Count on U to bring the deal home. Keep your chin up when others doubt U and betting against U. Be a cheerleader!

Do not make the age old mistake of thinking others are leaders and U are not. When it comes to your life U must lead! There are activities U must perform. One of the important ones is to sponsor self. That means put your money were your mouth is. U can not expect others to pay your way. It is the backbone of leadership to put one's money on the table in the pursuit of the dreams in one's heart. U have to put in the hard work, the long hours, and the sleepless nights. Lead by example! Don't go with your hand out looking for others to sponsor U when U have not proven that U believe in your own dreams.

Be prepared to give yourself the proper consequences for lack of performance. Don't get in the habit of letting yourself off of the hook when U know U failed to live up to your own standards. Consequences, timing, and skills are all activities of leadership. Get in front of your life and lead!

Listen 2U!

"Wisdom is the reward you get for a lifetime of listening when you'd have preferred to talk." --
Doug Larson

I was just saying...

Being an effective listener is a vital skill and a stepping stone to wisdom. How do U get all of the information available, by listening. So, the question is, how good of a listener are you? Please respond to each question, using 1=always, 2=frequently, 3=sometimes, 4=seldom, and 5=never.

1. I listen to what the speaker is saying and feeling?
2. I listen objectively?
3. I listen without judging the speaker?
4. I listen critically?
5. I listen for literal meaning?
6. I listen for the speaker's hidden meanings?
7. When the speaker is me, is the above true?

Wisdom is the outgrowth of listening. U understand self better when U listen to self. Your dreams become easier to visualize. It is easier to lead self when U listen to self.

I know U like to talk but it is not the better skill. Be careful, talking may get U in places U wish were never invented. It is better if U took time out to listen.

If U listen, mistakes can be avoided, consequences can be few, and U can sleep better at night. Listening is the sword of the wise. When U learn to listen U hear things that others miss. U learn to read between the lines. It puts U in a position to hear opportunities when they come knocking.

Talking has its time and place. When it comes your time to speak U will be able to do so with wisdom. People will listen longer, ask wiser questions, and debate with U less.

Listening sharpen your mental skills. U think things through. U problem-solve at higher levels. U use reason, observation and experience while planning future outcomes. U can develop, "if this, then that" action plans. People like U better when U listen to them. U will like self better when U can hear self think.

Ideas!

"Ideas are little rabbits. You get a couple and learn how to handle them, and pretty soon you have a dozen." -- Anonymous

I was just saying...

Ideas can frighten you. They can come in the middle of the night or driving home. Ideas are powerful. Have you ever had an idea knock U off your feet? Sure, you have! It can take on a life of its own, causing you to put the brakes on, thinking...let me get real.

You really have to learn how to handle thoughts that pop into your mind. Ideas teach you how to fly without wing, as Muhammad Ali puts it. An idea can make you feel like you just received a revelation.

I was in a meeting and a lady said, "I don't want to have an original thought ever." Everyone laughed but I sensed that she was not joking. She said it more then once, "Just tell me what to do and I will do it." It was clear to me that she had not learned how to handle ideas. They frighten her; therefore she was more comfortable being led, than being the leader, even in her own life.

Learn to write ideas down. Brainstorm on paper or with a recorder. Don't allow ideas to skip though your head without leaving a trace. Stop, listen and repeat the idea to capture it. Relax and allow yourself to experience the emotions, the sense of flying without wings. Once you know what to expect from the power of an idea, you will be able to handle a dozen of them.

Once U bring one idea into being U feel confident that U can handle another one. Before U know U have five or more balls in the air. U find yourself multi-tasking. Ideas are popping into your head by the dozens.

Ideas can give U the courage to do things U never thought possible, or beyond your skill level or U had been afraid of doing all of your life. But be careful, before U know it U will have 2 or 3 dozen rabbits...I mean ideas.

Dreams R Seeds!

I was just saying...

Dreams are like seeds, both need plenty of water, sunlight and fertile ground to give it a chance of survival.

All seeds are not alike, nor are dreams. Some seeds produce blades of grass, while others have an oak tree within. Dreams may produce small results or big results, regardless of the results, U should give them a chance to happen. Normally seeds need water, sunlight, and soil to reach its full potential.

The soil of dreams is the human heart. Your Heart is the soil from which dreams spring forth. Life experiences, environments, and imagination give the heart its fertility. The soil of the heart is enriched by worldly and spiritual matters. The more the heart can inhale from its journey, the more fertile the soil from which your dreams will spring from.

Dreams are watered from two sources, belief and commitment. Both water the dream, giving it a chance of survival. If U fail to commit to the dream it will only be a fleeting thought. The water of belief help dreams take root. Without roots dreams die. It cannot anchor itself in the heart, the soil, nor develop the muscle to push up through the soil without rain drops of belief and commitment. U will never know what is hidden within your seed, if U do not give it a chance to see the light of day.

If all U have is grass seeds, the roots do not have to be that deep. If by chance U have a Redwood tree, it will require strong commitment, conviction, and belief beyond measure to give it the roots it needs to maximize its potential. Most dreams are rotting in the ground, your heart for lack of water. Give your dreams a chance to survive by watering your garden with commitment and belief. Let there be rain! Let there be light!

Assuming U have the right soil and plenty of water, your dreams will see the light of day. Sunlight feeds plant life. Dreams need information, knowledge, and rational thinking to fully cultivate itself to full age. The mind, brain power eventually must be empowered. Imagination, ideas, and innovation are forms of light that give dreams a chance of happening. If U fail to research, investigate, and inquire, your dream's growth may be stunted.

Light is essential! Technology, higher education, and exploration are all forms of light. It is how dreams manifest and transform into reality. What once was a vision, a dream, a seed in the heart, now, behold, it is reality!

Cultivation of the heart, firm belief, commitment, and intellectual advancements is the soil, water, and sunlight of dreams. Give dreams a chance to happen!

Take A Risk!

"Behold the turtle. He only makes progress when he sticks his head out." -- James B. Conant

I was just saying...

Risk normally brings to mind failure, hurt or lose. Risk is not a negative word, it is positive energy. Risk is the catalyst for self-discovery, growth, and progress. Those who take risk gain more than those who sit at home. U can envy people who take risk because they become grand as the Grand Canyon.

Life does not become enriched by living in a shell or a self make prison. What U want is outside your comfort zone. At some point in time U are going to have to leave this place and move out. Stick your head out in order to see what the possibilities are. When opportunity knocks, open the door wide and venture outside.

Risk is a part of life. It enriches U! There is a difference in taking a risk and being risky. Risk is observation, planning, and goal setting. Risk is figuring out as many of the unknowns as possible. Examining different scenarios and the likely outcomes from option A verses option B. Risk is setting up safe guards, writing emergency plans, and listening.

Risky is living life by the roll of the dice. Risky is going which ever way the wind is blowing in the morning. Risky is being involved in illegal activities, get rich quick schemes, and shady dealings. Risky is playing in traffic, when U should be on the sidewalk.

There is a risk just walking down the street but walking in the middle of the street is a risky lifestyle choice. Risky are those Jackass videos stunts. Don't stick you head out for that. U will be better off staying in your self-made prison or comfort zone.

When U stick your head out U should have some idea what to expect if U did your homework. Businesses do their homework before opening at a certain location. They don't just buy the first vacant lot they come across, that would be risky. Employers don't hire the first warm body through the door. There is an interview process, job qualifications, and background checks. They take a risk in hiring U but the process removes risky decision-making.

U should do your homework, set up processes, and do not answer every knock at the door. Risk is part of life but U can minimize the danger, steer clear of potholes, and investigate opportunities before U spend your life savings. Avoid risky behavior!

Progress is obtained by sticking your head out. Don't let the thought of risk frighten you. You only get what you strive for. When the last time what U wanted just fell into your lap? Striving, movement, and risk are all necessary in the pursuit 2BU! U have to risk being U. Who U want to be is a risk U will have to take to find U. Don't hide behind artificial clothes, fake hair dos, or cookie cutter lives.

Dare 2BU! Take the risk. Dare to discover. Dare to stick your head out and put your feet on the ground.

R U Insecure!

"Success can make you go one of two ways. It can make you a prima donna, or it can smooth the edges, take away the insecurities, and let the nice things come out." -- Barbara Walters

I was just saying...

I spoke with a man who was successful, but insecure. He felt threaten in the workplace and at home. Success had not given him peace. It had not smoothed out the rough edges.

How U define success will most likely determine how it will impact your life. If succeeding is about cars, houses, and money, obtaining it may not give U the feeling U really need. These things can lead to arrogance and a life of show and tell. The question is who R U without all of these things?

When I looked at his "I love me" wall behind his desk, his insecurities stood out. His need to remind self and others he was "somebody." I was impressed, but the wall didn't make him a better person. It made him vain with no peace within. The wall blinded visitors to his insecurities.

Success is an okay pursuit in life but it is not the summit, the Mount Everest in the search of U. If U really want to avoid being a prima donna, then discover the things that bring U peace, smooth your edges, and bring nice things out of U.

It is said, "Money will make you the person you really are." Money may help you find yourself, but will you like yourself.

Another saying is "Don't believe your own press release." All of the flowery words and glamour pictures may fool the public but U know the real U, so chill. Don't fall victim to your own press release or your "I Love Me!" wall. Yes, U are accomplished, but your need to impress the little man is a sign of insecurities.

Success is a great thing, but make sure it is grooming you in the right direction. Are you becoming a better person? Are your edges smooth? Do others see nice things coming out of you?

Success has its price but the price should not be selling your soul to the devil. Real honest success is all about the person U grow into, not the material things, the lofty positions, or the house on the hill. If U find out U R a prima donna, success was not worth the journey.

Vastness of the Heart!

"Nobody has ever measured, not even poets, how much the heart can hold." -- Zelda Fitzgerald

I was just saying...

Lead with your heart! Your heart is deeper than all of the seven seas combined. Your heart is as vast as the universe. In your heart has been deposited your purpose, your dreams and your talents (gifts) from God. Your gift is as unique as your fingerprint. Your true potential is bottled up in the heart.

The Power 2BU! unlocks the treasures of your heart. The more U discover about self, the more access to the divine gifts, talents and potential behind the doors of the heart. Doors open if U practice a life of enrichment.

The heart holds The Power 2BU! It is the center of U. It enriches the entire body, mind, and spirit. Love, passion, desires, and emotions all are tied to the heart. How do U know your passions, if U do not know your heart. What do U desire? How do U gain mastery over evil desires if U fail to know thy self, which is to know your heart.

Success without self-knowledge is a heartless form of success. It is a smash and grab lifestyle or approach to life. U are left empty, without purpose when U fail to operate from the heart. Depression is well known among people who are rich and famous with everything but are like the lion, in Wizard of Oz, "if only I had a heart" they would have the Power

2BNew! Courage is essential, if U lack courage 2BU! your heart suffers the most.

Potential is energy at rest. Know matter how much you dream, plan, and make decisions about your future, nothing will happen until there is motion, kinetic energy. The heart holds the energy U need 2BU! Explore the heart! Ask it questions! Listen to it!

U will never exhaust the heart's capacity to discover, dream and design your destiny. It holds the hints to your destiny. Purpose is not hard to find if U go to the heart humble, respect its spiritual potential, and honor its divine gifts. It will guide to gardens unknown.

You do not have enough imagination to exhaust the capacity of your heart. Nor can you muster up more desire than the heart can handle. Your dreams may frighten you, but not your heart. Your heart is dream ready, it can do more than pump blood through your veins, it has the vastness of dreams, enthusiasm, forgiveness, and The Power 2BU!

Fifty-Fifty Chance!

"You may be disappointed if you fail, but you are doomed if you don't try." -- Beverly Sills

I was just saying...

U may be overcome by the thought of failure and everybody looking at U down in the dirt. If U don't try U will be known as the person who could not cut the mustard. U R damned if U do and damned if don't, if this is your approach to success.

There is one fact U need to be aware of; failure and success are byproducts of the same process, seeking The Power 2BU! When U try at anything the possibility of failure is equal to the probability of being successful. U have a 50-50 chance of either one. Trying is not the problem.

Not trying is your enemy! U are doomed if U just sit on the sidelines. The only way to increase your chances of success is to play the game. Play it at your peak performance. Don't come dragging in late for practice, then only give 10 percent. Life will only get harder. Success will appear as a mirage as if U were walking in the desert.

Don't be afraid to give life your all everyday. The more you except success the better you will become at planning, thinking, and acting in ways that increase the odds of success. Some people talk about succeeding, but their lack of planning, poor judgment, and risky lifestyle has failure written all over their efforts. Trying is one half but you must also perform!

Performance is the other half of the game. It is what turns the odds in favor of success. The more U perform, the more the percentage of success swings in your direction. Before U know it the odds of success will be 90-10. When success becomes a habit, your performance level will increase. When U look up, U will have an invitation to the final four. If U play the game smart, U will be standing in the winner circle, being crowned and handed the trophy.

The next time you are faced with the thought of failure, just remember the odds are 50-50 if you try, but 100 percent in favor of failure if you don't.

Attend The Power 2BU!™
Program or Sponsor One!

Join the hundreds of participants who have enriched their lives through one of The Power 2BU! Programs. The Power 2BU! is designed for individuals around twelve constructs:

   a) Fear
   b) Belief
   c) Attitude
   d) Success
   e) Destiny
   f) Excuses
   g) Courage
   h) Freedom
   i) Resilience
   j) Cultivation
   k) Leadership
   l) Spirituality
   m) Determination

It is time U Discover, Dream, and Design an individual Destiny. This powerful, motivating, and inspiring program leaves no excuses 2BU! and inspire U to ask and answer the "What if, What should be, and What will be" questions. U Can & U Will make the impossible possible. Come causal, suited, or laid back, all asked...U keep it real!

To attend or arrange a program in your area visit
www.thepower2bu.com

Join Our Mailing List

The Power 2B1NLove!™

This is not a "my marriage is in trouble" session. While it could help, it is about the destiny of the union. What do we want for us? Where should we be a year from here? And beyond! Establish a clear vision of why "We are in this love together!" This is a couple only, group session, facilitated to help both of U Discover, Dream, and Design your very own 2B1NLove Destiny! The ten construct are:

- Love
- Family
- Dreams
- Wellness
- Freedom
- Romance
- Friendship
- Spirituality
- Commitment
- Communication

The Power 2B1NLove! allow couples to develop a clear vision of their love together. Establish a 2Bodies1Soul partnership allowing U to create a 2Hearts1Dream Plan. Discover your communication styles and learn how spiritual matters enrich the ability 2B1NLove! Establish a wellness plan to live out your destiny 2B1NLove!

To attend or arrange a program in your area visit

www.thepower2bu.com

Join Our Mailing List

The Power 2B1Team!™

Performance is hampered by group dynamics which impede progress and results. Teams have to problem-solve, make decisions, and withstand setbacks. The Power 2B1Team is designed to coach and facilitate teams/groups to perform at peak skill level, take responsibility and be accountable collectively for their performance. A No More Excuse Attitude is developed as an approach to team performance. Built around eight constructs:

- Power
- Attitude
- Leadership
- Performance
- Communication
- Conflict Resolution
- Strategic Thinking
- Project Management

The goal is to give teams real tools which lead to effective team management, commitment to performance, and the resilience 2B1Team! Learn how to clarify functions, roles, and leadership. Solve immediate group dynamics facing the team. This is ideal for management, board retreats, departments, strategic thinking or MLM Teams or newly formed teams.

To attend or arrange a program in your area visit
www.thepower2bu.com
Join Our Mailing List

The Power 2BRMX4Life!™

Young men who want a fresh start or want to fine tune their game, The Power 2BRMX! is designed 4U. If U want 2RMX your life, RMX your game plan, or RMX your attitude to get more out of life, then this is 4U!   R U running the streets, maybe the streets running U?   Baby mama drama? Is incarceration in your future...if U don't RMX!   Don't wait 'till its 2Late! The 10 RMX constructs are:

- ➔ Manhood
- ➔ Women
- ➔ Choices
- ➔ Control
- ➔ Money
- ➔ Careers
- ➔ Dreams
- ➔ Principles
- ➔ Education
- ➔ Spirituality
- ➔ Entrepreneurship

Young men join the RMX party!   Develop the skills 2 beat the streets, avoid banging and slinging.   Learn how 2 get that paper (money), be a man 4Life, and handle baby mama drama.   RMX your game before the game RMX U!

To attend or arrange a program in your area visit
www.thepower2bu.com

Join Our Mailing List

I Want My Life Back!™

This program is designed for those behind bars, the recently released or those living risky lives. Life got U twisted, doing time, or caught in a revolving door. This program is your invitation to take your life back! The twelve constructs are:

- → Fear
- → Behavior
- → Success
- → Character
- → Choices
- → Conflict
- → Control
- → Resilience
- → Freedom
- → Dreams
- → Spirituality
- → Destiny

This is an action oriented workshop designed to give U the tools to beat the odds, embrace freedom and accept responsibility for your lifestyle choices. U will learn how to discover, dream and design your destiny. If U R serious and want your life back then you have found what U have been hoping and wishing for.

To attend or arrange a program in your area visit

www.IWantMyLifeBack.org

Join Our Mailing List

Thank U!